SALES SHOCK!

SALES SHOCK!

The End of Selling Products
The Rise of CoManaging Customers

MACK HANAN

Author of Consultative Selling™

amacom

American Management Association

New York • Atlanta • Boston • Chicago • Kansas City • San Francisco • Washington, D.C.
Brussels • Mexico City • Tokyo • Toronto

Library of Congress Cataloging-in-Publication Data

Hanan, Mack.
    Sales shock! : the end of selling products, the rise of comanaging
customers / Mack Hanan.
      p.   cm.
   Includes index.
   ISBN 0-8144-0248-8 (hardcover)
   1. Selling. 2. Sales management. I. Title.
HF5438.25.H3523   1996
   658.8'1—dc20   95-49738
                                              CIP

Printing number

10 9 8 7 6 5 4 3 2 1

Other AMACOM Titles by Mack Hanan

Consultative Selling™: The Hanan Formula for High Margin Sales at High Levels, Fifth Edition, 1995

Consultative Budgeting: How to Get the Funds You Need From Tight-Fisted Management, 1994

Manage Like You Own It: Take-Charge Strategies for Empowered Managers, 1994

Profits Without Products: How to Transform Your Product Business Into a Service, 1992

Growth Partnering: How to Build Your Company's Profits by Building Customer Profits, 1992

Competing on Value: How to Know Your Value, Price Your Value, and Sell Your Value (with Peter Karp), 1991

Tomorrow's Competition: The Next Generation of Growth Strategies, 1991

Key Account Selling: How to Gain Account Control With Major Customers, 1989

Customer Satisfaction: How to Maximize, Measure, and Market Your Company's "Ultimate Product" (with Peter Karp), 1989

Recompetitive Strategies: How to Regain Growth Profits for Mature Businesses, 1986

To Tsumbu Vangu,
    A missionary salesman in the Congo River
region of Zaire, Africa—a final refuge for vendors.
One day, at the edge of the rapids,
    The dugout canoe in which he makes
His sales calls struck a rock. A growing
    Pool of water swamped his merchandise.
The boatmen seemed to be losing their
    Struggle against the current carrying
Them toward the waterfall. Unfazed,
    Vangu nudged the passenger next to him
And said: "You know, if you don't mind a
    Little dampness and have patience for
Things to dry out a bit, I can give you
    A once-in-a-lifetime deal." Eyeing the
Waterfall, he added: "This offer cannot
    Be repeated."

Contents

Preface

Goodbye, Mr. Sales
or
Do You Remember Where
You Were Standing
When the Paradigm Shifted?

"When did you first notice your shortness of margins?" one of the Specialists asked the patient, a man named Sales.

"Lately, every time I discount," Sales said. "Looking back, though, it probably started five or ten years ago. I remember the office nurse telling me I had acute margin insufficiency. She told me to cut back on discounting. I was a heavy discounter: five times a day, every day, for years. Every year a few more percentage points. When the pain got worse, I thought it was a normal consequence of maturity. So I let it go."

"This pain, where do you feel it?" another Specialist asked.

"It comes on as a sensation I think of as The Squeeze. It gets me right between my costs and my prices. It used to be dull and persistent so I could live with it. Now it's so sharp sometimes that I can't discount anymore. It's gotten worse as my costs have gone up and my prices have had to come down."

"Your records show that you joined Cost-Watchers a few years ago," the Specialist with the thickest glasses said. "Consultants were called in. They put you on strict cost control. What happened?"

"It helped for a while," Sales said. "I even became the low-cost supplier two years in a row. But my costs got so low they couldn't support my cash flow. It became sluggish. Sometimes it stopped for days. I wasn't competitive anymore. So I had to generate more revenues. When I went out and sold, the costs came back. So did my shortness of margins."

The Specialists conferred. It had gone too far, one speculated. It is irreversible. Without margins, another said, his R&D is being deprived of nourishment. If profits fall, how will his new products get funded? His manufacturing will be unable to afford re-engineering. Key processes will go unrestructured. Unless there is continuous improvement, quality will suffer. When that happens, customer satisfaction—his last lifeline—will drop below acceptable levels.

"All you have to do is look at the indicators," said the Specialist with the off-centered tie. "Take any one of his critical success factors: his revenue-to-investment ratio. See how it's skewed all the way over to the investment side. His cost of sales is unacceptable. Take profits-to-revenues. Even when sales go up, they cannot produce enough earnings to replace his persistent weight loss on the profit side of the ledger. I give him a year or so as a viable presence in the marketplace."

"Three at the most," another Specialist said.

"Your optimism is based on nostalgia, not reality," he was told. "Only if Sales gives up going out to sell and goes on complete bed rest would I give him half that time. Let him sell from home."

"With bed rest, his circulation among customers will drop to zero. Where will his cash flow come from?"

"But he will have lower costs."

"Then, at best, he will break even. His ROI will be a straight line. Clinically, he will be dead."

"What if we implant a modem? He can sell by computer. Or we can hook him up to a telemarketing machine. He can get around with a couple of catalogs and go direct."

"What about third parties: value-added resellers, agents, distributors, or dealers? Can't they act as nurses' aides for him?"

When all the costs and benefits had been compared, nothing worked. The costs were always greater than the benefits. "I think we've come up empty," a Specialist said. "That is why I give him only a year or so. In that time, he will still be functional. But his decline will be progressive. One day, he will simply run out of margin entirely. He will have complete margin shutdown. The more volume he goes for to try to make up for his margins, the more it will cost him. He will simply sell himself into the grave."

Unnoticed by the Specialists, and they would have ignored her even if they had noticed, Mrs. Sales sat off by herself. We grew up together, she mused. He preferred childhood games to girls—chasing smokestacks, ringing doorbells, asking people if they were open to buy. Even in high school, he was always busy making calls that got results. In downtimes, he would pump himself up to sell harder. When that didn't work, he would sell smarter. Nothing stopped him. He would even sell conceptually if he had to, whether he knew what it meant or not. If the truth were known, he preferred to sell strategically. But he could be prevailed upon to consider his customers' personal agendas and fill out colored pages analyzing their innermost predilections. No matter how busy, he was always gracious enough to stop long enough to overcome an objection.

Mrs. Sales trailed off in her musings. The Specialists packed their charts and diagrams and filed out, already calculating their invoices.

A cat scan they left behind showed that Sales had been, quite literally, hollowed out. His earnings had been scooped from him as if by a giant ladle so only the shell of his revenues remained. Perhaps, Mrs. Sales thought, she should call Missing Persons. She could make a case for it: Sales had disappeared. Somehow, probably through nervous dialing, she got the Safe & Loft Squad instead. Who had motive and opportunity? the top cop asked, reading from a cue card. They all looked at each other. They knew. Their lips moved in unison: *the customer.*

Sales's customers did him in when they mandated open standards, which they then set. You want to sell to us? they asked. Okay, no more proprietary products. Everything must meet the same standards. That way, we can buy from anyone.

And once we can buy from anyone, we no longer have to buy from everyone. Why bother? Things equal to the same things are equal to each other. At that point, Sales's products had become instant commodities. In a single stroke they had become marginless. His customers could forget features and benefits. As long as a supplier met their specifications—their standards—they could buy on price. Lowest price.

Without having to buy from everyone, Sales's customers cut back on their purchasing managers in the same ratio that they cut back on the number of suppliers they continued to do business with. Sales would go for days without finding anyone to make a pitch to. He wore out several sales cycles just this way alone.

It would not have mattered what business Sales was in. If he had sold packaged goods to supermarkets, customers would have set his standards just as industrial customers were doing. They would have told him: This is how much of each product we will stock—right down to each size and flavor—and here is the stocking and shelving allowances we require, here are the deals and discounts, and here are the promotional allowances. Is it a new product? Here is the guarantee you must give us in case it dies on the shelf.

From the Halfway House where they moved him, still wearing his "Born to Sell" T-shirt, Sales thought to the last that he would be back on the street the next day, doing business as usual. Mrs. Sales, a woman with midwestern values that are becoming harder to find, had the decency to withhold from him the latest company directive that put all sales reps on a profit-based compensation plan instead of volume. That would have been too much. The intent was certainly commendable. But where would the profits come from?

Still, it all had a Twilight Zone feel to it. Sales's products were better than they had ever been. Topnotch quality. Almost zero defects. Made by best practices. Delivered just-in-time. Yet, somehow when you added it all up, you got everything but margins. It was almost like a paradigm had shifted. Somehow, Mrs. Sales felt, I don't think we're in the 1980s any more.

Part I

Choosing Your Business Model

How to Restyle Your Organization for the End of Selling

1

The Era of SalesWorld 2000

The second half of the 1990s is your "Last Chance Saloon"—your fast-closing window of opportunity to answer the single most important question affecting your business: *What kind of sales function should we have?*

You start out knowing two things:

1. Your answer will be different from any answer you would have given at any time before. The old models, including the way you are selling now, are dead. If you try to put lip rouge and eye makeup on them, they will look better by the candlelight of your requiem for the end of selling, but they will still be dead.
2. If you do not answer, the role of low-margin commodity supplier will be imposed on you by default.

There is a three-step thought process you must go through to get to your answer:

1. You must determine what kind of business strategy you want your sales function to serve.
2. In order to know that, you must first determine what kind of business strategies your major customers and clients are planning through the year 2000 so that your strategy can be compatible with theirs.
3. Then you can determine what kind of sales organization and selling operations are most likely to add the maxi-

mum value in the most cost-effective manner to your customers' business strategies.

The question you ask first—about your kind of sales function—turns out to be the question you answer last because your sales function must "report" to your customers' and clients' objectives. It must be engineered as a subset of their own strategies. Its standard of performance must be continuously to improve your customers' ability to realize their objectives.

This new way of looking at the positioning of your sales function—that it must move profits, not just products and services, to your customers—is what *sales shock* is all about. Figure 1-1 shows the step change that marks the end of the old sales model and the beginning of the new one.

On the far side of the fault line between the old and new worlds of selling is SalesWorld 2000, a world where sales forces are no longer necessary or affordable; where multivendor shopping is no longer cost-effective; where customers and their suppliers are no longer separate and distinct; where price is no longer a sales tool or a purchase decision; and where 99 and 44/100ths percent of today's sales training is no longer relevant.

SalesWorld 2000 announces the fact that selling has proved

Figure 1-1. Step change.

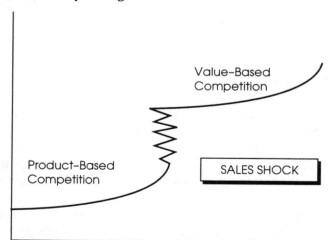

to be a failed concept. As the spearhead function that was supposed to make a business customer-driven, customer-oriented, and customer-focused, selling has instead made companies technology-driven, product-and-process-oriented, and self-focused on "our products," "our features and benefits," and "our differentiation from our competitors."

The greatest failure of traditional selling strategy has been its concept as a closed fist to wage warfare against competition instead of an open hand to extend partnership to customers. In order to partner, you cannot sell *to* a customer. You must sell *with* him and *for* him so that you can achieve shared objectives—improving the customer's competitiveness—shared strategies, and shared rewards. To use selling to "kill the competition" or to use sales forces as "hunters" to stalk unwary customers and as "skinners" when they have been ambushed is a bastardization of its proper competence.

Comparing Added Value to Added Cost

The new world of SalesWorld 2000 is a far cry from worlds that have preceded it, such as Ken Olsen's DEC-World, Digital Equipment's annual computer exhibition. In 1990, amid falling profits, Olsen took the blame for his company's misplaced focus on what his customers really wanted. "We were selling computers," he said, "while customers wanted solutions to business problems. You can see at DEC-World that we've addressed that." But DEC-World was then, as it had always been, "a showcase of innovative technology." Even though each innovation was presented as a solution to a business problem, customers knew that their problems were dollar problems and that solutions also had to be expressed as dollars and not bits, bytes, and bauds. It took no time at all for customers to figure out that Digital was still selling computers.

The transition from technology-based sales to value-based sales is revolutionizing the way business is being carried on. It is a true revolution. In just ten years, the onset of SalesWorld 2000 can be seen in Digital's industry by comparing the results of *Sales & Marketing Management* magazine's 1984 survey of "the best sales forces" with their 1994 status. Each company appears in its 1984 rank order followed by its 1994 updating:

1. *IBM*—undergoing massive sales force downsizing and business divestitures
2. *Wang*—being born again with a downsized sales force after re-organization
3. *Hewlett-Packard*—concentrating sales through third parties after undergoing companywide massive sales force downsizing
4. *Burroughs*—merged with Sperry, ranked number six, and re-organized as UNISYS after undergoing companywide sales force downsizing and business divestitures
5. *Digital Equipment*—concentrating sales through third parties after undergoing massive sales force downsizing and business divestitures

The end of selling has been the single most important operating change of the past three decades. It first came to notice, as Figure 1-2 shows, at the Dawn of Commodity Realization when the prevalent type of sales representatives—a class of product sellers colloquially known as "boxmen"—began to be deprived of margins by the increasing sameness of their features and benefits. As differentiation became vestigial, along with it went the reason-for-being of a human sales force: face-to-face demonstration of product uniqueness.

In SalesWorld 2000, the decision to supply human labor content to the sales function is being made on the answer to two questions:

1. How much value does a human seller add? This is answerable by the difference he or she makes in margin.
2. How much does the added value cost? This is answerable by the seller's fully burdened cost of sales.

The net result of comparing added value to added cost is a rate of return on the investment in a human seller. This can be compared with the rates of return from investments in alternate

Figure 1-2. Sales Darwinism.

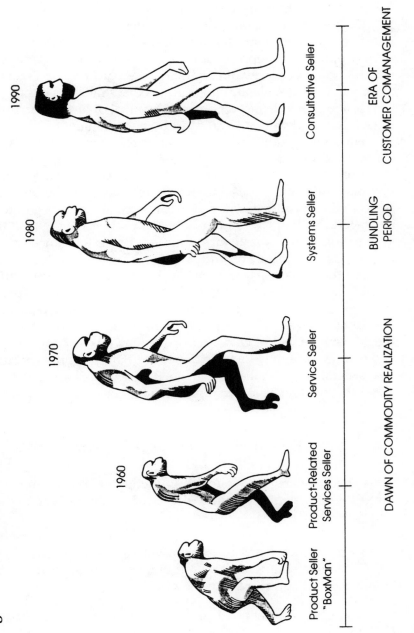

Product Seller "BoxMan"

Product-Related Services Seller

1960

Service Seller

1970

Systems Seller

1980

Consultative Seller

1990

DAWN OF COMMODITY REALIZATION

BUNDLING PERIOD

ERA OF CUSTOMER COMANAGEMENT

distribution strategies that require no people at all or that can use people on other organizations' payrolls.

Customers are asking the same questions about their suppliers' sales forces. Wal-Mart's answer is to refuse to do business with supplier sales representatives. In this way, the commissions that the salespeople would ordinarily be paid can be deducted from the costs of each supplier's goods that Wal-Mart has to pay. This is a merchandising version of a reversal of fortune: Supplier sales forces add value to Wal-Mart by not selling.

For a generation and more, sales forces were trapped in the stasis of adding greater and greater value to their products instead of adding value to their customers. This inward-looking box mentality was persistent, even extending into the bundling period when products and product-related services began to be packaged together. No matter how comprehensive the resulting system, a product was always central to its performance specifications, its nomenclature, and its price.

All the while, however, as Darwinian survival of the fittest would have it, a second branch of sellers known as profit-improvers was splitting off from the hunter-skinners. Their "product" was enhanced cash flows for their customers through the comanagement of customer operations whose contributions to customer profits were to be improved. These are the consultative sellers, the comanagers of the 1990s, who have outstrategized the product sellers and made them obsolete.

Re-Engineering the Sales Process

Sales shock means that your sales function of the near-term future—the time period of SalesWorld 2000—must adhere to three criteria:*

1. Your sales plans must be a subplot of your customers' business plans so that your business can be positioned as a profit contributor to their businesses.

*For a fuller discussion of near-term future sales models, see Mack Hanan, *Tomorrow's Competition*, AMACOM, 1991.

2. Your sales strategies must accelerate customer business strategies so that your business can be operated as a co-manager of their businesses.
3. Your sales objectives must be the result of adding value to customer business objectives so that your business can claim a partner's right to share in the business growth you help add.

By re-engineering the historical sales process, sales shock has caused disharmonic vibrations in bread-and-butter strategies like these:

- Manufacturing everything you sell
- Selling only what you manufacture
- Accumulating market share without regard to profitability
- Fielding a nonindustry-specific horizontal sales force that sells anything to anybody
- Selling with only a direct sales force
- Compensating a sales force for volume
- Adversarial selling
- Pricing products and services

As organization structures have been modernized by shrinking and flattening, as businesses have become virtual, and as middle management support functions have become automated, the sales function has been regressing instead of moving forward. Selling cycles have grown longer, costs of sales have grown higher, discounts have grown deeper, and margins have grown fewer and further between even as sales volume has risen. In the final quarter of John Aker's chairmanship of IBM, a record sales volume yielded a record multimillion-dollar loss. For IBM, as well as for Sears, Kodak, General Motors, Exxon, and just about every other business in the Fortune 500, sales have not been keeping up with corporate reformation.

Sell-harder sales strategy has put businesses at more risk than reward. Sales forces, both in staffing and training as well as in their sense of mission, have added more to cost than value. So have sales support services, compensation schedules, and organization schemes. Marketing has become an anachronism. Sales managers have become vestigial. Sales, as typically planned, practiced, and paid for, have lost their power to make businesses grow to their new restructured potential.

As it became clear that neither selling harder nor selling smarter was going to have much of a curative impact on margin depreciation, sellers began to sweeten their deals with what they called value-added services or value-adds.

Depending on the customer, value-adds could include extended warranties, priority repair services, stretched-out payment terms, and free training. Whether or not any of these services actually added value—after all, no one knew their value any more than they knew the value of their products—they certainly added costs and further discounted the original product margins.

When this became apparent—that value-added services were really price discounts in sheep's clothing—and it was suggested that customers pay something for them even if it was just to break even, it was pointed out that customers had already been educated to expect them to be free. In this way, product-related services were on their way to becoming every bit as much commodities as the products they were intended to brand. There was nothing left that could command a margin.

Exploding Suppliers Into Two Tiers

SalesWorld 2000's sales function is becoming polarized between a small Tier 1 class of consultative comanagers and a larger Tier 2 mass of vendors. Their different modes look like this:

Tier 1 Consultative Comanagers

Option 1: Provide service only
   - Systems integrator
   - Continuous process improver
   - Facility/category comanager
Option 2: Provide service and self-made products

Option 3: Provide service, self-made products, and multi-vendor products and services

Tier 2 Vendors

Option 1: Sell self-made products and services
Option 2: Sell self-made and multivendor products and services

Figure 1-3 shows the traditional Enterprise business model that most of today's managers have grown up with but that, in SalesWorld 2000, has exploded into its two tiers because it has

Figure 1-3. SalesWorld 2000 business models.

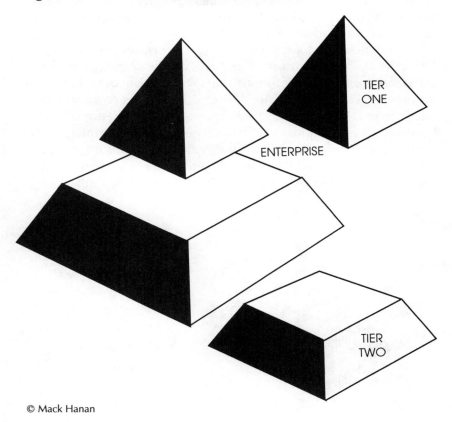

© Mack Hanan

become nonfunctional as a margin-making machine. Once believing that its two types of capital, intellectual and physical, could synergize each other, it eventually has had to come to terms with their endless civil wars. Centrifugally, each has now gone off on its on. Tier 1, the pyramidless peak of the old Enterprise, has become an intellectual capitalist—a pure play of human intellects. Conversely, Tier 2 is a peakless pyramid that contains the Enterprise's manufacturing and processing capabilities. Tier 2 is a physical capitalist.

Tier 1 operates as a general contractor, distributing any products and services it may make along with related multivendor products and services to its customer-clients with whom it consults on the application, implementation, education, and evaluation of their contributions to improved profits. Tier 1 has no sales force. It does not need sellers because it does not sell. Instead, it comanages client operations. Figure 1-4 takes you inside the Tier 1 model.

Tier 2 is a Tier 1 supplier. Tier 1 intermediates between Tier 2 and the end users who are Tier 1 clients. Tier 2 makes products and services, supplementing its lines with products and services from other Tier 2s. Like Tier 1, Tier 2 is moving toward a zero sales force. It does not need sellers because it does not sell. Tier 1 buys from Tier 2 under cost-certain contracts as a strategic ally, acting as purchaser for its customer-clients. A sales force would add more to a Tier 2's cost, and therefore to price, than to value and would nullify the cost-certain basis for its Tier 1 alliances.

Figure 1-4. Inside Tier 1.

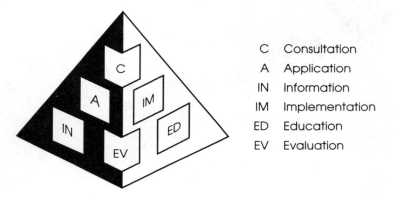

C	Consultation
A	Application
IN	Information
IM	Implementation
ED	Education
EV	Evaluation

Hewlett-Packard, which was once an Enterprise, is on the way to becoming a prototypical Tier 2. Its Enterprise model exploded because "The HP Way," its founders' philosophy of doing business, set two of the company's values against each other. In one, the Way said that "We achieve our common objectives through teamwork"; in the other, the Way said that "We encourage flexibility and innovation." When Bob Frankenberg, a general manager who represented HP's intellectual capital, wanted to get an innovation approved, he had to deal with thirty-eight in-house teams on everything from product features and benefits to product launch locations. In order to sanctify the name "New Wave" for a software product, one hundred people on nine teams took seven months. This burden of "decision overhead" was commonplace in Enterprises whose intellectual capital was subjugated by the Total Quality Control philosophy of engineer-driven manufacturing businesses where hardware capital always comes first.

The Tier 2 peakless pyramid shows what remains of the basic manufacturing company model as the result of trending away from vertical integration. The Tier 1 model, in contrast, owes its existence to the equal and opposite trend to subcontracting and outsourcing. In each case, managers are fleeing unnecessary costs.

SalesWorld 2000 is evolving into a costless and risk-free world. No customer wants to take on a supplier's costs by acquiring inventory. Nor do customers want to take on the risk that a supplier's products or services may turn out to be sunk costs rather than returnable investments. In a world dominated by a zero-cost, zero-risk mentality, traditional vendor selling strategy would only add to cost and risk without compensatory added value.

Figure 1-5 takes you into the Tier 2 model, which is principally a manufacturer's model whose contrasts are obvious with the service provider's model of Tier 1.

Living in a World of Alternatives

The new SalesWorld 2000 models of Tier 1 and Tier 2 are ending the role of sales as the major way that suppliers and their cus-

Figure 1-5. Inside Tier 2.

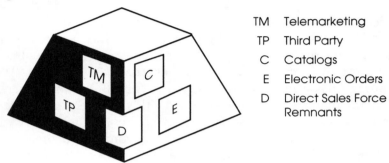

TM   Telemarketing
TP   Third Party
C   Catalogs
E   Electronic Orders
D   Direct Sales Force
     Remnants

tomers do business with each other. In SalesWorld 2000, the key word in the transmutation of selling is *alternate*. Selling's successors are all alternatives to the established sales process. In earlier years, they were spoken of as alternatives to the mainline sales culture symbolized by the direct sales force. SalesWorld 2000 represents a 180-degree change. Direct selling has become the diminishing alternative to comanagement, third-party sales, telemarketing, and all the other forms of distribution that are superseding it.

Businesses in every industry are finding alternative means of leapfrogging their physical delivery systems. Even "personal service businesses" are substituting impersonal services for traditional sales forces. Banks once thought of themselves as the most personal of service businesses since they dealt with their customers' money, something that would not casually be trusted to machines. Yet automated teller machines (ATMs) and telephone banking are progressively replacing walk-in branch offices. Most banks have set up telephone banking services under the name "Direct"—Chase Direct, for example—as separate banking entities. Short of depositing and withdrawing cash, banks are finding that anything that can be done in a branch can be handled over the phone. They are also finding that it can be handled for almost two-thirds its former cost.

For Tier 1, selling is a superfluous alternative. Consulting skills and business partnership strategies practiced with mid-level customer operating managers are the prerequisites for comanagement, not feature and benefit presentations offered to techno-purchasers. For Tier 2, selling is an unaffordable alternative as a delivery system for price and an unnecessary alternative for working under single-sourced contracts to Tier 1.

Accordingly, Tier 2 is addressing its needs for cost control to its sales forces in the same way that it is divesting unnecessary expenses from all its operations. *Automate* with labor substitutes and extenders, Tier 2 managers are saying. *Delegate* to outsourced labor, and *migrate* indispensable labor out from under corporate overhead.

- Automate in the form of Electronic Data Interchange (EDI) order entry and inventory management, by faxing bids in response to faxed RFQs, and by soliciting sales with electronic and hard-copy catalogs and advertising on the information superhighway.
- Delegate in the form of downloading sales to third-party resellers and other distributors such as dealers and agents.
- Migrate in the form of spinning out internal sales forces to work in their homes, cars, and customer offices and plants.

All by itself, automation is going a long way to advance the end of selling.

- By 1995, J. C. Penney was already selling over 1,000 of its products electronically, without ever having a customer come into a store or a salesperson asking "Can I help you?" The store itself may be next to go.
- Fleet Financial Group has replaced hundreds of its people who used to sell credit cards, home equity, and auto loans by processing the applications they once handled with a software program that gives a go/no-go for each loan when it finishes processing. The software works faster, cheaper, and more accurately than people.
- Pacific Gas & Electric has automated the first stages of its sales process where new electric service installations must be designed and their costs estimated. Its sales force of 500 is progressively being downsized.
- Coca-Cola is eliminating its salespeople who visit vending

machines to check on sales and restock. The machines are programmed to report their own sales daily, hourly if need be, and to reorder new stock.

The negative impact of automation on sales forces attests that SalesWorld 2000 is a good deal more than a latter-day remake of Arthur Miller's *Death of a Salesman*. Miller wrote in the singular. He was salesman-specific. SalesWorld 2000 is generic, replacing all sellers everywhere in the shift of value away from selling physical capital to applying intellectual capital. The value shift that is displacing sellers is having the same impact on their customers. The ultimate reasons that "no salesman will call" will eventually be because no buyers remain to be called on.

The call itself has become an anachronism. A venerable institution, the call has brought vendors together with their buyers in the traditional confrontational stance of facing off against each other across the buyers' desks. Sometimes the call had a sales purpose; more often it did not, serving instead as a reconnaissance to scout out latent needs or lurking competitors, or simply to keep communications open and memories fresh. But whatever else it did, it ran up a cost for both sides.

In the latter half of the 1980s, it became possible to make calls remotely, with consultative sellers and their customers interacting through real-time software programs like Mack Hanan's PIPWARE™ CloseMaster™—PIP for Profit Improvement Proposal™—which enables successive what-if options to be created, evaluated, mixed, and matched in microseconds.* Physical proximity was made unnecessary. Players could be anywhere. Play could be anytime. As a result, sales became closable at high margins and customer profits became improved at high values that make the margins justifiable.

Choosing Your Model

What kind of alternative sales function do you want to operate? You have two choices:

*PIPWARE CloseMaster and Profit Improvement Proposal (PIP) are registered trademarks of Mack Hanan. All rights reserved.

1. If you want to be a Tier 1, you must be among the most cost-effective product and service mixers who can create optimal systems, apply them for superior results, and take leadership in realizing the most improved outcomes from their application. Your alternative to selling is to operate as a consultant in profit-improving outcomes.

2. If you want to be a Tier 2 supplier to Tier 1, you must be able to apply technology to your own business in order to be a low-cost manufacturer of standardized products or a low-cost, high-volume provider of standardized services. Your alternative to selling will be to operate as a telemarketer, cataloguer, or third-party supplier. Through EDI, you can receive and acknowledge purchase orders and send invoices and shipping notices from computer to computer as well as computer-aided design diagrams of products that customers want you to make for them, all without human contacts on either side.

Where are you now? You can assess your current positioning, which reveals how your customers are dealing with you rather than how you think they are or how you might like them to, by counting how many times you say "That's us" to the following ten qualifiers:

1. If your customers maintain a data base of their vendors' "normal prices" for common solutions and your solutions are included, you are a Tier 2.
2. If your customers maintain a "vendor template" that they apply to your product performance and service capabilities and your products and services are included, you are a Tier 2.
3. If your customers restrict your access to "normal channels" within their purchasing organizations, you are a Tier 2.
4. If your customers prefer to tour your facilities instead of touring your norms for improving their profits, you are a Tier 2.
5. If your customers make a distinction between "our best interests" and "your interests" and suspect that you

may be more interested in creating business opportunities for yourself than for them, you are a Tier 2.

6. If your customers warn you about "no surprises" in what you bill them for or how much you bill, you are a Tier 2.

7. If your customers invite you to "exceed customer expectations" but do not reward you for your contributions of added value by gainsharing with you, you are a Tier 2.

8. If your customers do not know your value, measure your value, or pay you for the value you add to their operations, you are a Tier 2.

9. If you get into a squeeze and want to raise prices and your customers tell you that they will go to someone else—as J. R. Derickson, CEO of Hiwasse Manufacturing Company found out when he asked for an 8 percent price increase and "You would have thought I had asked for their firstborn the way they hollered"—you are a Tier 2.

10. If your customers compliment you on your positive attitude in negotiating discounts in order to arrive at "fair market prices," you are a Tier 2.

Putting a Value on Human Touch

"Human touch" has become the critical success factor in SalesWorld 2000:

- In order to be a Tier 1, you must touch the customer last in a consultative role. *Tier 1 is hands-on.*
- In order to be a profitable Tier 2, you must reduce the number of people who touch each product and you must reduce the amount of time each of them touches it, whether they make it or sell it. *Tier 2 is hands-off.*

In Tier 1, touch conveys added value because one human being touches the plans, policies, and programs of another. But in Tier 2, touch adds unrecoverable cost whenever a human being touches a product in a replaceable manner—replaceable by alternatives whose assets are either lower cost or cost nothing because they are on someone else's books.

SalesWorld 2000 transactions at Tier 1 are manager to manager, not seller to buyer or vendor to purchaser. They are based on an exchange of financial values in the form of mutually improved profits: higher earnings from better revenues or lowered costs for customer managers in exchange for higher margins and lowered costs for their provider comanagers who co-create them.

Taking leadership of this sort of value exchange, which means coming up with a steady state of profit-improvement projects and comanaging their results, requires the skills of an asset manager and the mindset of either a profit center or cost center operating manager. These are not traditional sales skills. Either they must be taught as part of a Tier 1 conversion process from vendor to consultative seller, or managers who already possess them must be acquired.

Selling and all its hard-core strategies—features and benefits presentations, cost-based pricing, overcoming objections, trial closing, and making the cuts—has migrated into mutual asset management at the middle-manager level. For customer managers who run profit-centered lines of business, comanagement of their profit-improvement projects has become Tier 1's primary growth strategy. Customer managers who run cost-centered business functions have their cost-reduction projects comanaged. In order to grow their own businesses, the new generation of postsellers has come to understand that they must first generate a revenue source by growing the businesses of their customers.

In their role as customers, managers have come to the realization that the consolidation of their industries into two or, at most, three major competitors means that it is going to be increasingly difficult from now on for them to grow by continuous expansion. The only workable strategy is to grow by continuous improvement in their profits based on ever-increasing operating competitiveness. There is only so much that any customer can do on his own. Doing it alone also confers risks. You can miss out on a new curve. Or you can fall behind on an old curve and not find out about it until it is too late.

In a competitive environment where no customer needs more than a single major supplier for each operating category of his or her business, customers need all the help they can get to be the preferred suppliers in their own industries. This makes their Tier 1 comanagers indispensable as an outsourced staff. For Tier 1, it also makes Tier 2 indispensable as outsourced suppliers.

In SalesWorld 2000, Tier 1 and Tier 2 share this symbiotic relationship.

Figure 1-6 shows how they network with each other to maximize value to Tier 1's customer clients and, through them, to their clients' customers. Throughout the network, there is one common denominator: there are no traditional sales forces to be found anywhere.

The networking of Tier 2 suppliers by each Tier 1 is analogous to the colonization of supplier-type nations by the former Great Powers, where each power dominated a sphere of influence that ensured its access to vital resources and allowed it to obtain them on most-favored-nation terms. Tier 1s are coming to be known by the colonies they keep as strategic allies, joint venturers, growth partners, and other forms of virtual organization. Tier 2s, in turn, are becoming known by the powers that keep them.

Doing Business in a Commodity World

The self-interest of all end-user customers is to impose commoditization on continuously higher levels of product performance. The same is true for product-related services. Customers commoditize by issuing or enforcing minimal standards of acceptability that form SalesWorld's barriers to entry for invitations to bid. If you meet the minimal standards, you can bid. If not, you become a nonplayer.

When all suppliers are in compliance with the same set of standards, they become equal to the same things and therefore equal to each other. SalesWorld 2000 is a commodity world.

Figure 1-6. Value-added network.

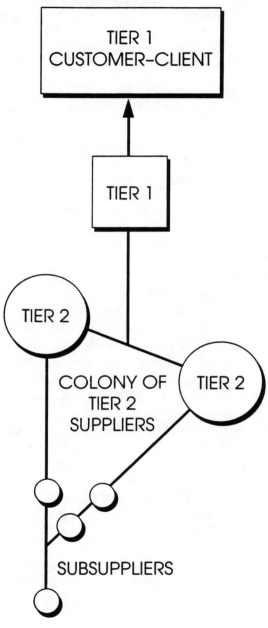

By commoditizing their supply sources, customers reduce the job of their purchasing functions to the rote issuance of requests for price quotations since specifications are already legislated at the lowest common denominator. In some cases, customers may ask for something more: an itemization of free related services. RFQs like these can be generated by computer, distributed by fax or E-mail, and evaluated by software, all requiring few touches by human hands or interventions by human minds.

Under imposed commoditization, differentation becomes a deviation from standards of performance. Instead of making a supplier more attractive, it rules him out if he is substandard and gives him no credit toward a higher margin even if he exceeds standards. Either way, the supplier is out of compliance. If extra benefits were deemed necessary or desirable, they would have been included in the standards.

Being a commodity supplier is apparently mesmerizing. Over and above the provocation put forth by standards to "comply or die," Tier 2s are gratuitously self-commoditizing their operations. They are in headlong pursuit of "best practices," their industry's most cost-effective operations. Their pursuit leads to imitation, where every supplier in an industry wants to have the lowest workflow costs and highest productivity along with the shortest cycle times. Everyone wants to be as quick to market as the best practitioner who is first to market. Everyone wants to fulfill as many orders the same day they are received as the best practitioner in same-day order fulfilment. As best practices become institutionalized as parity practices, each industry of Tier 2s becomes a producer of commodity products by means of commodity operations.

In each industry, Tier 2s are replicas of each other. This helps them avoid costs by eliminating the need for sales and marketing functions. But at the same time, it multiplies their vulnerability to easy replacement.

As interchangeable parts of their Tier 1 supply colonies, Tier 2s live on the edge of transience. Increasingly, combinations in either real or virtual forms attract them as a survival option.

2

The End of the Traditional Sales Force

Since the mid-1980s, sales forces have been on the way out. In some cases, their extinction is being accomplished by eviction. Branch offices are being closed and their staffs are working out of homes, cars, and customers' offices, or being spun off as outsourced distributors for their former parents. In other cases, sales forces are being replaced by technology, either computers or telecommunications, or by third parties whose very name as "value-added resellers" announces the reason for their existence.

Sales forces are vanishing because few traditionally managed suppliers can justify a customer's line-item audit of their pricing structures.

As product and service commoditization has become commonplace in one industry after another, sales forces have been relegated to being mere distributors of price, for a long time their sole remaining differentiator. But in SalesWorld 2000, price is no longer being set by suppliers. This has taken away their sales forces' last "product," leaving them nothing to sell.

The PICOS program of General Motors shows how supplier sales forces are being made irrelevant by abrogating their pricing option. PICOS stands for GM's Program for the Improvement and Cost Optimization of Suppliers—cost optimization being a politically correct term for the continuous cost reduction of all the parts that go into making each car.

GM is committed to the proposition that each part's price must be a function of the total target price of its cars. This means that the price of a seat, for example, is no longer a reflection of its supplier's cost plus a fair profit. Instead, GM decides arbitrarily that seat prices must be reduced by 20 percent if the cars that the seats go into are to be competitive in their market segments.

José López was the chief perpetrator of PICOS. He gave his name to what became known as the López Line, a six-point program of price management:

1. Overall Strategy
   a. Get immediate price reductions (please remember that two-thirds of GM's European profit was generated by price reductions we got from our suppliers).
   b. Secure longer-term price reductions from all suppliers.
   c. Sort out the first and second tier suppliers.
   d. Only single source with significant price reductions (18 to 40 percent) that are firmly baked into fixed price, long-term contracts.

2. Tactical Overview
   a. Establish well-qualified, well-trained, and articulate purchasing clones in all business units to implement these practices.
   b. Plan extensive supplier price reductions for each car model.
   c. Send out inquiries around the world in search of the lowest unit price.
   d. Establish short- and long-term price reduction targets and go very low.
   e. Know your potential winning suppliers and their competitors inside and out before you begin to negotiate and play first and second tier suppliers against each other.

3. The Underlying Themes
   a. Identify and parade the enemy as Japanese companies, not GM.
   b. Understand the balance of power between each supplier and GM.

      c. Keep taking the temperature with vendor ratings and supplier council meetings.

      d. Offer exaggerated growth and future order quantities as bonuses.

      e. Start working with the likely winning suppliers as early as possible on price reductions that are termed "cost reduction improvements."

4. Before Awarding the Deals

      a. Establish long-term contracts as the ultimate goal.

      b. Establish the long-term contract rules.

      c. Establish that nonprice factors like tooling costs and R&D are not allowed.

      d. Resist all suggestions that some supplier costs are not controllable (i.e., raw materials).

      e. Focus all activity on dramatically and immediately reducing the unit price.

5. The Agreements

      a. Tie up the short-term unit price.

      b. Keep nibbling away at the price and terms even at the midnight hour.

      c. Always appear to be in a desperate hurry, but in reality take as much time as needed.

      d. Pull the long-term deal out of the cupboard.

      e. Intensely squeeze some more out.

      f. Get the supplier to sign.

6. Managing the Chosen Suppliers

      a. Introduce the suppliers to our corporate commodity councils and our advanced purchasing product development teams.

      b. Totally involve each supplier's top and upper management—get commitments that the supplier's middle management would never make.

      c. Request that each supplier provide you with detailed information on the cost-profit structure of the products it currently or proposes to sell us.

      d. Don't accept raw material indexes as cost information

when a supplier proposes a price increase; get the cost-profit information.

e. Establish a friend-buddy relationship with middle- and lower-level supplier people to pass cost-profit and competitive information to us.

f. Be prepared indirectly and under pressure to bluff and lie.

g. Destabilize each supplier's people with many urgent meetings and many demands for information.

h. Set new deadlines for suppliers to meet but defer decisions to increase their anxiety.

A GM supplier confronted with being "Lópezed" has three choices: comply, capitulate to GM's consultants who will help reorganize his manufacturing process, or cast about for a replacement customer who is not on PICOS but can promise equivalent volume.

The answer is not Chrysler. Not only is Chrysler smaller. It also has a "score" to settle with its suppliers. Score stands for Supplier Cost Reduction Effort, a mandatory program of cooperation with Chrysler to cut supplier prices a minimum of 20 percent across the board.

The triple bogey of low cost, high quality, and high productivity—three objectives that are antithetical to each other—is forcing suppliers to trade off the cost of sales in preference for automation, outsourced subsuppliers, and re-engineered organization and operations. These sales force-less businesses are the Tier 2 companies of SalesWorld 2000.

Geon, a B. F. Goodrich division, is a case history of how a business gets to Tier 2, which represents its survival state. As a producer of polyvinyl chloride resin, a commodity, Geon was on the high end of overhead costs. When it was faced with coping with its customers' PICOS-type programs, it had to sacrifice margins first, R&D second, headquarters staff third, plants fourth, and the sales force fifth, along with outsourcing its truck fleet operations, warehouses, payroll, and accounts payable, and reducing the number of raw materials that go into its products by 75 percent.

SalesWorld 2000 assumes a universal equality of product

and service quality: in other words, mass commoditization at customer-satisfactory levels. With quality standardized, price has remained the only exposed variable. In order to eliminate all variables, customers are deciding how much they will pay so that price, like customer standards, becomes commoditized. Customers have been saying for a long time that they have not needed a supplier's sales force to distribute price. In SalesWorld 2000, customers have removed price—and, along with it, customer sales forces—from the distribution channel.

The focal point of Tier 2 strategy is to be *cost-controlled* so that Tier 1 strategy, to be *cost-certain*, can be served. Every unnecessary dollar of a Tier 2's working capital must therefore be cut back, especially dollars locked up in the short-term fixed costs of a sales force.

At the beginning of the century, a manufacturing business like Geon could get by with allocating as much as fifteen cents from each dollar of sales as working capital. By the mid-1990s, fifteen cents had shrunk by two-thirds to five cents on the dollar and was still going down. In order to operate in such a capital-controlled environment, a Tier 2 business must manufacture its products under demand flow, which means nothing gets made until a customer orders it. It must keep close to zero inventory on hand so that financing can be managed without borrowing. It must maintain zero defects standards so that goods can go out the door as soon as they are finished and not come back. And it must be able to sell without a sales force.

Being Chosen the Preferred Supplier

In the interests of cost containment, Tier 1s are taking a consolidated approach to procurement by reducing the total number of their suppliers. If not a single source, two preferred suppliers are being selected in each category of a Tier 1's needs who are capable of providing high-quality products and high levels of service at everyday low prices. Once they are selected, preferred suppliers are put under long-term contracts in return for progressive improvements in quality and productivity, accompanied by step-by-step price reductions. Honda was happy with a

2 percent annual price break up to 1994. As an example of a Tier 2's cost of doing business in SalesWorld 2000, Honda raised it to 3 percent for suppliers who want to stay on its list.

Some of a supplier's lost price comes out of margins. The rest must come from a mix of continuous improvements in labor efficiency, economics of scale from long runs of standardized parts, and strict waste management based on a no-inspection, no-rejects policy.

Tier 1s consult regularly with their Tier 2 suppliers to help them find ways to achieve continuous cost reduction. They get paid for their counsel by the lower prices their Tier 2s can give them as a result of a reduced cost base. A Tier 1 that practices "strategic sourcing" by turning over product design or assembly to a Tier 2 will implement its practice with counsel on re-engineering the Tier 2's order fulfilment process so that it operates on a codependent cycle time with Tier 1's customer needs. It charges no fee for the counsel. It makes it up in zero inventory carrying costs.

Under this regime, Tier 2s have no selling expenses. There are no requests for proposals to bid on. Traditional show-and-tell sales calls are made unnecessary. Almost everything is pre-sourced. For its Cirrus and Stratus compact sedans, Chrysler chose 95 percent of their parts suppliers before the parts had been designed.

In addition to trading off margins as their dues for being selected, Chrysler's preferred suppliers have been required to create further economies by acting as contractors for the subsuppliers who support them. The subs, in turn, have to cut their own costs in order to qualify. At the same time, though, they must take on new expenses from managing inventory, making multiple just-in-time shipments, and designing and engineering components that were once pre-designed for them.

José López, first at General Motors and then at Volkswagen, has become the founding father of merciless margin-squeezing of Tier 2 suppliers by their Tier 1s. At GM in 1992, López and his purchasing team of self-styled "warriors" sucked in their cheeks and cloaked the messy business of downsizing supplier profits in the selfless quasireligious mission statement of "creating more value for the customer" through lower prices. But

"You can't cut prices and raise productivity forever," one Tier 2 component maker said of the López "continual improvement process." When a manufacturer could cut-and-raise no further, he was given an F for failure on the litmus test of being a loyal GM supplier based on unwillingness to enlist in the value mission.

Wal-Mart is to retailing what General Motors is to North American automobile manufacturing. What Wal-Mart wants, Wal-Mart gets, as Black & Decker learned with its Quantum line of power tools. "The whole point behind this product line," B&D said, "is to have it driven to market by what the consumers really want." Yet, when Quantum came to be marketed at Wal-Mart, it was the distributor and not the customer who set its price ceiling at $100. This told Black & Decker who its customer had been all along and where it should have started its market research.

Wal-Mart also had to tell 3M who its customer was for 3M's consumer products. Process-driven and product-focused since its inception, 3M is a classic Tier 2 industrial vendor. Its consumer products group is an orphan. For years, it had been shipping out truckloads of one hundred-sheet Post-it notepads because one hundred was a nice round number. Wal-Mart knew better, having sized up its shoppers as needing only 42 or 67 sheets. Its message to 3M was, "We don't want it anymore the way that you're giving it to us."

Being a preferred supplier means never having to say that you are out of stock. Hewlett-Packard is positioning itself to be every Tier 1's dream supplier, making itself into an information products utility. HP visualizes itself as a one-stop source of building-block types of "information appliances" like PCs, digital devices that compute as well as telecommunicate and fax and print, and other low-priced, high-performance commodities for business and personal use.

HP's Wal-Martization of information products can be achieved only by a high rate of innovation turnover. It is an expensive game to play. It is also perilous. A single miscue that misjudges or misses a cycle of innovation can mean disaster. When IBM's PC business misjudged its market's demand in 1994, it lost $1 billion in sales and 6 percent of its share. Even when a Tier 2 avoids mistakes, each new product has only a small window of opportunity to make money. As Kevin Bohren of Compaq Computer has said, "It used to be every new product had six months of uniqueness. Now it's a long weekend."

Selection as a preferred supplier conveys a single right—the right to appear on a Tier 1's "open to bid" list. This guarantees nothing; it simply allows a Tier 2 to bid when requested. Requests are influenced by a Tier 2's willingness to provide "free goods" over and above its products and services. When General Electric Acceptance Corporation went shopping for accounting services, it made clear that it expected more than high levels of professional service at the most cost-effective pricing structure by asking for several Tier 1-like "little extras" thrown in for good measure:

1. Ideas for creative value-added solutions to problems standing in the way of GEAC business goals.
2. Insights into GEAC's business that express a supplier's experience and expertise.
3. "Outside the box" strategies that can result in continuous revenue increases and cost containment for GEAC.

Offsetting Shrinking Margins

Throughout the 1980s, Enterprise-type businesses had been constantly struggling for earnings despite gross profit margins of 40 to 50 percent. In industries where cost of sales was a major contributor to total operating expenses, it was often a critical success factor for profitability. When Enterprises atomized into the Tier 2 model and divested their sales forces, they had more to show on their bottom lines for the value of their technologies even at margins that were less than half of what they had previously been pulling down.

Product and service demarginalization is global. No one can escape it. "How do you assign prices in a world where quality is perfect?" asks Yotaro Suzuki of the Japan Institute of Office Automation. If the world is SalesWorld 2000, Hiroshi Yamauchi of Nintendo has the answer: "There is no way to charge a premium on hardware."

As the technology component that "informs" products increases, two results become generic to all product lines. One is that quality is equalized. The other is that performance is also equalized. The cost to build it in cannot be recovered by the price that can be charged for it. When technology has no upward impact on a product's total price, it therefore cannot be sold.

Tier 2 managers never see a cost they can afford to like. Sales costs stick out. Managers torment themselves by asking:

- When technology can no longer be priced, who needs a sales force to sell it?
- When quality is equalized, who needs a sales force to sell it?
- When products and services can no longer be differentiated by quality or performance, who needs a sales force to sell their sameness?

Undifferentiated high-performance, high-quality products can be sold only in Tier 2 by one of three survival models:

1. The C-Cube Model, where you get to market first and "run as fast as you can for as long as you can" until someone catches up and passes you or the race is over.
2. The Dell Model, where you customize your commodities so that no two Dell computers are alike no matter how many Dell computers there are.
3. The Intel/Microsoft Model, where you own the standard of product performance that gives your commodities a brand.

Each model relies on high-volume, low-cost productivity. It also relies on markets that are growing faster than prices are declining. If the two curves touch, the end game begins.

When technology and quality lose their uniqueness, a sales force to sell them loses its value. Without differentiation, demonstration is meaningless. Distinctions without a difference are additionally without meaning. Men and women paid to make them add only to cost.

Tier 2 managers have no choice but to become experts in cost control, productivity, and inventory management. They live or die on pennies of cost and minutes of cycle time like the differences between spending 17.5 cents or 22.5 cents of every sales dollar on contribution to overhead or turning inventory 4.5 times a year instead of 3.9.

Hewlett-Packard's baptism into Tier 2 came through its PC business, whose workforce had to be cut from 4,000 to 2,200, more than half of them in sales, so it could show a profit at gross margins below 20 percent. Even so, sales had to be increased by at least 15 percent every year just to maintain a constant contribution to profits. Sales at this rate could be achieved only by "desperation discounting." As a consequence, volume went one way while contribution margin went the other.

Dell Computer, an HP competitor, sells almost entirely through an 800-number telephone network and mail order catalog. Each of Dell's computers is customized, built from standardized parts only as ordered. Assembly is mostly outsourced to contract manufacturers. Delivery to Tier 1 is made by mail, ready to be plugged in with operating system software and applications programs that are already loaded and lifetime support guaranteed. Dell customers never see a salesperson. At most, they see an expert repairman but only if a hot-line telefixer is unable to get a customer back up and running.

Making Every Penny Count

The smallest uncontrolled cost or price competition from even lower cost suppliers can make Dell's Tier 2 formula unworkable. IBM made that discovery when it tried to go head to head with Dell by creating a clone in its Ambra Computing Corporation. Ambra was set up as a stand-alone subsidiary that planned, designed, and developed low-cost computer systems. Ambra had no in-house manufacturing capacity. It had no sales force and did not even staff telemarketers, outsourcing 800-number sales to a third-party ordertaker and processor.

Yet, no matter how low it priced, Ambra was never able to become a preferred supplier. Dell or some other Dell sell-alike was always able to offer technology that was just as good or even better at a lower price. Ambra was abandoned by its market on its first birthday.

Living with everyday low margins, not many Tier 2s can make money without an operating model that makes every penny count. Lear Seating has learned this lesson the hard way. Ford has concentrated its orders for car seats with Lear and a small number of other suppliers. In return, Ford expects annual price reductions of 5 percent a year. "They're squeezing us," Lear's CEO Ken Way says. "It hurts, but if you don't like it get out of the business."

Lear stays in business by using its capital with extraordinary efficiency, letting as little of it as possible get tied up so it can maintain a return on equity of 30 percent. But there is no chance that Lear can go on playing this game forever. Its future profitability as a Tier 2 depends on helping its Tier 1 customers save money in other ways than discounting Lear's prices. One strategy is to become a supplier of integrated systems composed of seats, door and instrument panels, and ceiling insulation. Lear took the first step in this direction when it acquired a manufacturer of automobile interiors. This has made it more attractive to its customer, enabling Ford to reduce its supplier base by one. It has also given Lear a broader base against which it can try to play off Ford's annual demand for givebacks in price and giveaways in service.

As the Lear example shows, competitive pricing is dependent on a Tier 2's ability to manage its operating costs: speeding up cycle times to improve rates of response, consolidating functions to get rid of redundant costs, and keeping inventories low.

Size makes no difference. Boeing could fit Lear into a corner. But in order to win the competition for a $1.2 billion airliner order, Boeing had to cut its $35 million asking price per plane by one-third to match the lowball $22 million bid from McDonnell Douglas. Boeing's morning after the win was devoted to cutting its manfacturing costs by 30 percent over 5 years without harming engineering or development of increased fuel efficiency or safety. Even so, the 30 percent cut may only help keep Boeing even with the price.

The problem begins here rather than ending. Southwest, American, British Airways, and the aircraft lessors immediately demanded the same break from Boeing. Even with manufacturing superproductivity, Boeing is already eating up to 3 percent of its costs as they escalate annually and looking to ship increasing amounts of work to cheaper Mexican and Asian suppliers. Boeing's CEO Frank Schrontz says, "It is no longer allowable to say, think, or believe that building airplanes is different."

When Tier 2s report their earnings, cost-effectiveness can account for two-thirds to three-quarters of their annual gross profit margins. By and large, they come from improvements in manufacturing, usually from automation that displaces labor, improved distribution logistics, a price squeeze on their suppliers of materials and components, and more economical inventory management. Average revenue per unit will rarely rise, putting immense pressure to push the number of units higher and higher.

Engineering-Out Costs or Passing Them Along

Tier 2 companies must follow a rigorous agenda to stay competitive. Regardless of their industry, the agenda always includes "standard industrial cost-efficiencies" like these:

- Peel layers of management.
- Hold down inventory.
- Improve just-in-time (JIT) delivery.
- Reduce time to market.
- Shorten production time.
- Reduce factory space.
- Increase revenue per employee.
- Decrease employment.
- Keep pay increases small and infrequent.
- Squeeze costs of employee benefits.
- Upgrade production technology.
- Replace sales force with EDI and telemarketing.

Caterpillar has adhered to the agenda by cutting its employment by 40 percent over 15 years, closing nine manufacturing plants and investing $1.8 billion to modernize its remaining factories, and almost doubling productivity since the mid-1980s.

Sun Microsystems has cut its production time from 90 to 10 days on many components of its workstations while reducing factory space by two-thirds. As a result of increasing output by five times, Sun has raised revenue per employee to $400,000 from $90,000 in 1989.

In their attempt to keep a tight grip on fixed costs, Tier 2s are in a running battle with making or buying. Too much of either brings problems. Some Tier 2s like Seagate Technologies make almost every piece-part of their products. Others follow the Sun Microsystems model and try to be hollow. Sun used to have outside suppliers manufacture and assemble its workstations. Contract shippers delivered them to customers. Its own employees never touched Sun's products. But Sun got stuck when suppliers could not "come up the volume ramp" fast enough. Sun had to fill in some of the hollowness with self-manufactured parts.

The unrelenting pressure to innovate forces damned-if-you-do, damned-if-you-don't choices on every Tier 2 business. If you move first to innovate before the next cycle of customer needs becomes obvious, you risk being wrong. The best time to launch an innovation is also the chanciest, when a market is in its infancy. The reward for correctly predicting an emerging need is in the margins and volume that come from being first to market. The penalty is in the fast cycling down of your transient monopoly from competitors who have been drawn to your market by the smell of money.

However, if you wait to see how many customers will ask to have an innovation before you go commercial with it, you may be too late to catch its curve at a price point that returns your investment at a profit.

Tier 2s must be managed for low risk. They have little room for error. Yet error is inevitable in the high-stakes guessing game of innovation. Too much too soon is bad enough. But too little too late is worse. You may recover from betting on a curve that never crests. You can always sell your inventory. But you may never recover from the opportunity costs in money and experience from a curve that is missed.

The moment that costs start to creep up, a Tier 2 manager is in trouble. The old escape valve of passing a rising breakeven point along to customers in the form of a price increase has been permanently foreclosed. Tier 2s have fallen back on two strategies:

1. The KFC (Kentucky Fried Chicken) approach is to "engineer out" increased costs by switching to lower cost suppliers, reducing packaging costs, or downscaling the ingredients in its recipes until breakeven comes back down again.

2. The Kingsbury approach is to "return the favor" of a mandated discount by passing it along to its own suppliers in a domino effect. When General Electric imposes a price reduction on Kingsbury, a producer of bearings for large machinery, Kingsbury imposes the same reduction on its Delaware Valley Steel service center. In turn, the service center passes the reduction along to the mills it buys from.

Playing With Cost and Price

The two models are generally successive. A Tier 2 tries the KFC approach as long as it can. Then it converts to the Kingsbury strategy. But the Kingsbury "value subtracting chain" is only as strong as its lowest breakeven supplier. After that, Tier 2s look to see how they can share costs through collaborations, strategic alliances, and joint ventures. Some Tier 2 partners share R&D. Others create common specifications that they hope will become industry standards, eliminating costly variations and reducing the number of model types they must purchase or manufacture and stock.

Once a coalition of Tier 2s can get their suppliers to agree on an industry standard, they can preconfigure their manufacturing and redesign their product lines to use commodity components. Purchases can then be made on the open market on the basis of price from many competing subcontractors. This keeps a Tier 2's costs down as well as enabling it to speed up reaction time to its Tier 1 customer's orders. Assured of low-cost supply, a Tier 2 also acquires the flexibility to avoid having to forecast and thereby risk being stuck with inventory by building its own products only as orders come in.

By making purchases just in time on the open market, Tier 2s relieve their subsuppliers of the need to sell to them. This replicates the way that Tier 2s are relieved of the need to sell to Tier 1, and for the same reasons. As sales forces are reduced or eliminated throughout the Tier 2 supply chain, costs can be brought down even more. Breakeven comes down with them and so can the prices within each Tier 2 network as well as the prices charged to Tier 1s.

In the Tier 2 model, breakeven is a critical success factor. Keeping it continuously dropping is one of a Tier 2 manager's key performance indicators. The race is between lowering breakeven faster than the next cycle of discounted margins can overtake it. A 3 percent discount off a $1 price may not seem too much for a Tier 2 to pay for a renewed contract. But if its costs remain at 91.9 percent, the profit on 97 cents instead of $1 falls from 8.1 percent to 5.1 percent—a 37 percent loss.

"Making it up on volume" is often held out as an inducement to discount. But higher volume can never offset lower margins. Because variable costs go up with increased volume—the "costs of volume" that offset the economies of scale—sales must rise between 10 and 15 percent just to get a Tier 2 back to where it was before a 3 percent price cut. As a rule, unit costs are stubborn. They generally refuse to fall until sales increase at least 20 percent. Since each price cut of 3 percent can be expected to produce at most a 5 to 6 percent increase in volume, it takes four discount cycles to get to 20 percent.

Gross margin is the place that Tier 2s look for the interplay of breakeven cost and price. The percentage of sales that can be retained as profit tells a Tier 2 whether it is giving away margin beyond its means.

Compaq Computer combines cost constraint with discounted prices by following the rule of "more volume in less space with fewer people touching the product." In other words, it increases the number of personal computers it produces per employee per square foot of factory space. Compaq puts its rule to work with strategies like these:

• Converting its traditional assembly line operations to three-person work cells that subassemble component parts, assemble them into a computer, and test them within each work cell. Only three workers touch each product instead of the fifteen or so on an average assembly line. With every less touch, time and costs are saved and the chance for error is reduced. Work is speeded up to where it takes only fifteen minutes of human labor to assemble and test each computer. Under this system, employee output in each work cell has been increased by almost 25 percent.

• Building-to-order instead of trying to forecast demand. By making production dependent on actual orders, costs are saved at every step of the manufacturing-to-retail network for inventory handling, freight, and return of unsold goods. Obsolescence of parts is also reduced. The costs of forecasting are eliminated altogether. Margins can be retained as a result of customization on an order-by-order basis while the economies of mass production are preserved.

• Making more cost-effective use of people. Indirect labor in jobs like inspection and supervision can be reduced, with workers transferred to direct manufacturing. Compaq has gone from 1.10 support employees per line worker to 0.38, reducing its supervisor-to-worker ratio from 1:20 to 1:70. With more workers freed up, Compaq can run its factories twenty-four hours a day.

Divesting the Sales Force

Deprived of product or service differentiation, a Tier 2 company's competitive advantage is in the quality of its execution. Its proprietary skill set must be the way it manages its version of the Bermuda Triangle: *minimizing costs while optimizing quality and maximizing productivity,* as Figure 2-1 shows.

Tier 2's execution can be made cost-effective only by two

Figure 2-1. Tier 2 "Bermuda Triangle."

strategies. One is automation, which substitutes machines for human hands that are adding more cost than value. The second is outsourcing, which substitutes someone else's less costly human hands to add more value than cost.

Working within the Bermuda Triangle reveals the inherent incompatibility among its three forces. Maximizing productivity can raise costs. It can also reduce quality, as in the case of Hewlett-Packard's "shocking printers." In order to speed up productivity, HP increased automation on its OfficeJet lines. The hurried-up manufacturing process left metal slivers inside the printers' casings that caused electrical shocks when the particles touched the power supply.

Human hands add cost to everything they touch: every product, service, or process. As this truth is applied to the sales function of Tier 2 businesses, it is causing them to react with the same remedies—automate and intermediate. Automation is being accomplished by inbound and outbound telemarketing connected to direct-by-mail catalogs and by electronic data interchange where order entry is correlated with just-in-time inventory replenishment. For the rest, third-party intermediaries act as outsourced sellers and resellers.

Tier 1's purchasing function is becoming an EDI system or a fax machine. Figure 2-2 shows how Tier 2's sales function is evolving into a telemarketer and a catalog, along with third-party outsourcers who are dealers, distributors, manufacturers' representatives, or value-added resellers (VARs). The direct sales force and its correlate, customer purchasers, are going out of business together for the same reasons. Commoditization has made both of them unnecessary. Cost has made both of them unaffordable.

Sacrificing People to Breakeven

As Tier 2 businesses progressively divest their sales forces, they are following a two-step scenario:

Step 1: Downsize the sales force by eliminating the bottom 20 percent who call on nonkey accounts. Assign their customers

Figure 2-2. Tier 2 sales force evolution.

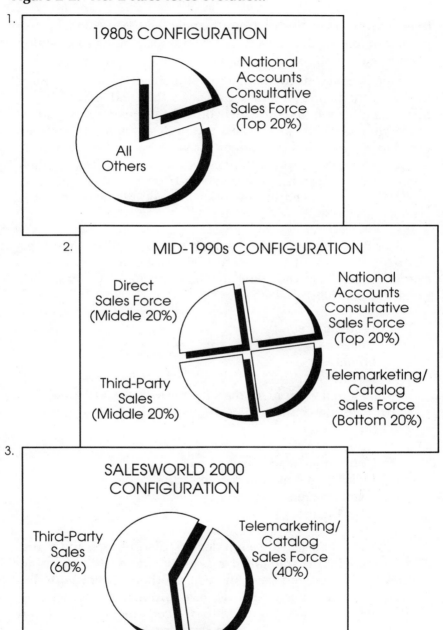

to telemarketers or third parties the way the IBM Personal Computer Company sells entirely by 800-number linked to a catalog of over one hundred products, many made by competitors.

Step 2: Spin out the remaining 80 percent of the sales force to reduce their contribution to overhead. IBM and AT&T are setting up halfway houses for their officeless sales representatives in warehouses with bare-walled, rent-a-desk "hotels" equipped with laptop ports and telephones. As withdrawal symptoms disappear, the sales representatives work from offices in their homes and cars as telecommuters and from their customers' offices. When they need to network, they socialize electronically around their e-Mail "water cooler."

Tier 2 businesses end up selling through indirect channels of distribution as alternatives to their own sales forces. As an example, Tier 2s in the computer industry have set up a wide range of "alternative sales forces":

1. Distributors
2. Dealers
3. Franchisers
4. Resellers
5. Original equipment manufacturers (OEMs)
6. Mass merchant retailers
7. Superstores
8. Consumer electronic stores
9. Company-owned chains
10. Private label manufacturers
11. Telemarketers
12. Direct mailers

When a Tier 2 sells through dealers, distributors, and value-added resellers, the tradeoff it makes is cost control versus account control. You can have one or the other but not both. Jim Graves, a Hewlett-Packard VAR, has summed it up this way: "HP never has to be introduced to our customers. We own our customer base." For HP's purposes, Jim Graves is their customer. For Graves's customers, Graves is their supplier. The Tier 2 mantra—make the highest quality product and sell it at the lowest possible price—is a recipe for bankruptcy if a single human hand adds a single dollar of unnecessary cost to a single operation of its manufacture or sale.

Selling at the lowest price does not require selling. Nor can selling on price sustain the seller's cost of sales. Since the only standard that quality needs to meet is acceptability, there is no meaningful differentiation to sell. Accordingly, there will soon be no one on the customer's side to sell to because there is no differentiation for the customer to buy.

Removing Selling From Acquisition

Selling is being removed from Tier 1's acquisition process because it no longer adds value greater than the costs to Tier 2 of fielding and supporting a sales force or the reciprocal costs to Tier 1 of staffing and housing a purchasing function to deal with vendor sales forces. Tier 1's minimum standards replace purchasing. They ensure homogenized quality within a predictable range of value. Selling adds no incremental value to the mix because commodities are not sold on value but are bought on price.

It has been a long time since even a best-of-breed sales representative has made a compelling difference in the Tier 2 sales equation. Competitive parity and the equality of quality have taken away his or her traditional appeals. At the same time, customer standards have negated proprietary selling propositions. The net result is higher sales costs and lower margins. Sales proposals that lose out in the end because price cannot be brought down any lower are an unrecoverable cost. Even the costs of sales that are closed may exceed their selling price.

When all the costs of a typical sale are added up, it is the sales representative's contribution that leads all the rest. Sales representatives who have been ignorant of the value of their offerings have imposed the most serious liability. They have only been able to communicate product specifications to customers—the antiquated features-and-benefits syndrome, a task more economically performed by a fax machine—and have left their customers in the dark about what impacts to expect on enhancing their revenues or reducing their costs.

Sales representatives have talked "increased productivity," but they have failed to quantify its value. Similarly, they have featured "ease of use," "low maintenance," "improved efficiency," "greater convenience," and the granddaddy of all clichés, "increased profitability," but have not been able to put compelling numbers against any of them. As a consequence, no value has been added to the customer dialog, making it an unrelieved cost.

The self-assessment of one Fortune 500 manufacturer sums it up succinctly for many of the other 499:

> There is a general consensus that our sales force does not understand our customers' needs for value. The sales force is still selling on technology first and its applied value last, if at all. Our ability to add value is a secret. None of our customers identify us as the value-adders we are because we have never made clear to them how our products and services can improve their businesses—how we can increase their revenues or decrease their costs and therefore expect to be compensated in kind. Our pricing model, which is based on cost-plus and competition, is as obsolete as our sales model.

Up to the 1990s, sales forces could get away with their costs because they were evaluated chiefly on their revenue-to-investment ratios. As long as they brought in more than they cost, they were all right. But as soon as companies had to become low-cost sellers as well as low-cost suppliers, the key ratio changed to investment-to-breakeven and the key question became: How much can breakeven be reduced when a sales representative goes off the payroll and his or her sales are brought in at a lower investment?

As Tier 2 businesses reallocate their sales forces, Figure 2-3 shows that they have three possible places to go. Two of them are outsourced, either to dealers, distributors, or manufacturers' representatives who have no manufacturing overhead, or to

Figure 2-3. Vendor sales force reallocation options.

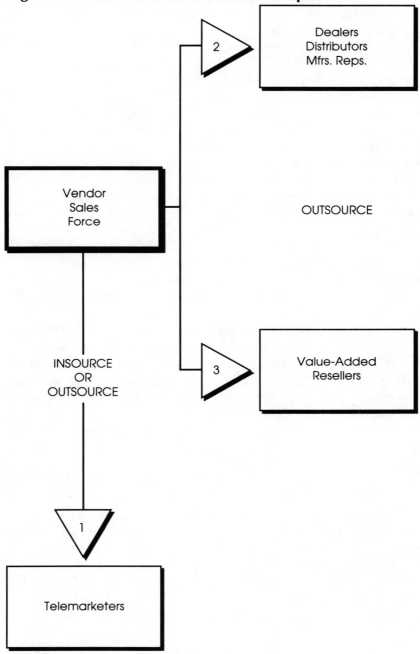

value-added resellers. The third place is to stay insourced as telemarketers, today's telephone-ringing versions of yesterday's doorbell-ringing smokestack chasers.

Peeling the Cost Artichoke

Standardization of product and service performance at good-enough levels of quality has had a significant effect on forcing reductions in Tier 2 purchasing, manufacturing, and employee training costs. Same-day order fulfilment and just-in-time management have had similar effects on reducing a Tier 2's inventory costs. EDI, telemarketing, and outsourcing sales to third parties are getting rid of personal selling costs. This progressive peeling of the cost artichoke leaves a Tier 2 with only its most necessary expenses—those that fund its core capabilities of R&D, product design and development, and manufacturing. It is this ability to concentrate its funds and avoid all expenses that are peripheral to them that enables Tier 2s to remain profitable under demarginization.

The unrelenting cost competition in Tier 2 is leading to a concentration of major suppliers that parallels the dominance of a few Tier 1s in each market. But the basis for their survival is different. Tier 2s that make it hold operating cost advantage. Taking expenses out of a product by shrinking its order entry, assembly and testing, and delivery from 5 to 3 days can be a matter of life or death. In Tier 1's value system, the supplier with the best track record for continuously improving Tier 1 profits becomes the supplier of choice.

Tier 2's self-interest in protecting its profits in the Tier 1-Tier 2 relationship simultaneously serves the self-interests of Tier 1 in two ways. By commoditizing products and services around predictable standards, Tier 2s enable Tier 1s to buy from them only on price. And by merging, as many Tier 2s are doing, to increase their purchasing power by taking advantage of volume pricing for themselves, they enable Tier 1s to deal with a smaller number of suppliers.

Within Tier 2, seven rules are emerging for competitive advantage:

1. Invest heavily in laboratory research to sustain the development of rapid-fire product variations, each with an incremental edge.
2. Go for mass markets to gain economies of scale or for high-margin niche markets.
3. Cut costs to the bone to keep cutting prices on new, improved product entries.
4. Upgrade technology before it matures instead of trying to squeeze every last cycle of contribution out of it.
5. Create well-engineered products of high quality that can support ironclad, lengthy warranties.
6. Flow back profits to make continuous improvements so that you "eat your young" before competitors can consume them.
7. The seventh rule has to do with selling without a sales force. It comes from the hard numbers of distributing discounted products and services when the delivery system is the traditional direct sales channel. It is supplemented by anecdotal evidence like this: "One of our best salespeople sold a $3 million order at a 54.75 percent discount. As his rationale, he told the customer that the price break coupled with free coop advertising funds, prepaid freight, and free services of a product trainer would 'elevate the customer's awareness of the benefits of doing business with us.' The salesperson wrote in his call report: *The customer practically sold himself.*"

As this kind of "aggressive selling" has become the rule rather than the exception, more and more customers have ended up selling themselves. As a result, fewer and fewer sales representatives have been needed to sell them. Among the Fortune 500, news releases like this are becoming increasingly common: "Procter & Gamble said it was replacing up to 500 full-time retail sales representatives with part-time, contract, and telemarketing personnel as part of its cost-saving efforts." Where there is no added value, there can be no added cost.

3

The Surge of
Comanagement Force

The surge of comanaging, and with it the end of the traditional sales force, is a recognition of the central fact of business in SalesWorld 2000. *Intellectual capital has become the only form of capital that bears sustainable margin value.*

No industry is immune to margin amputation from its products or services:

- In banking, fee income for managing stock, bond, and mutual fund portfolios is superseding interest income. Banks still make money on money. But transacting intellectual capital makes more money for a bank than moving financial capital around because it helps to make a customer's money more valuable instead of simply more secure or more accessible on demand.

- In health care, hardware- and software-based drug delivery systems are losing their margins to the ability to manage improved patient outcomes through in-home medication. Greater value is added to a hospital by discharging a patient to home care one day sooner rather than administering a drug 1 percent more accurately.

- In computers, the technology capital that researches and develops them no longer commands the value of intellectual capital that can apply them to make money or save money for their users. Margins on boxes and chips are clipped almost at introduction. Only nine months after Digital Equipment's Alpha

AXP microchip was introduced as being faster than a Cray supercomputer, it was giving away 30 percent of its price.

Tier 1s are capitalizers of their intellects, using them to apply financial and technology capital—money, products, services, and multivendor systems—to add value to their customer-clients' operations. Their outcome is *net realized value* (NRV), new money that a client can take to the bank as the return on his or her investment in Tier 1 intellect. As a result of their control of intellectual capital, Tier 1 businesses can act as comanagers of their customers' operations in SalesWorld 2000.

From their intermediary position between the customers they refer to as clients who are upstream from them and the Tier 2 suppliers who are downstream, Tier 1s work in two ways to adhere to the analects shown in Figure 3-1.

1. Upstream, Tier 1 proposes to clients the added values from its comanagement. Its proposals are outcome-specific, operation-specific, and application-specific. A comanager talks to a customer-client's manufacturing manager like this:

Figure 3-1. Tier 1 analects.

1. Make continuous improvements—not individual transactions.
2. Take the initiative—don't sit back and wait for requests.
3. Improve your customers' competitiveness—not your own selling strategy.
4. Teach customers how to apply—not what to buy.
5. Generate new revenues for customers—don't just cut their costs.
6. Add new values to customer results—not just new assets to customer inventories.
7. Develop customer businesses—don't focus on just developing your own.
8. Convert customers to clients—not just satisfied customers.
9. Make profit accumulation your major objective—not market share.
10. Empower your people with comanagement capability—not sales skills.

- Your current cycle time for product design is 2.5 thousand manhours. Our clients average 1.7. Ask me how we can partner to bring you closer to our norm. What if we can bring you one-half a manhour closer to start—how many dollars can we save from your current costs and how many new dollars can we realize from speeding up your sales?
- Your current cycle time for line changeovers is 72 minutes. Our clients average 40. Ask me how we can partner to bring you closer to our norm. What if we can bring you 12 minutes closer to start—how many dollars can we save from your current costs and how many new dollars can be realized from speeding up your sales?

2. Downstream, Tier 1 imposes on Tier 2 design-for-satisfaction and manufacture-for-satisfaction requirements, talking to a supplier's manufacturing manager like this:
   - Our standard for quality is a maximum of 86 imperfections in every one million units shipped. Unless you can improve your quality from your current 146 imperfections per million, you cannot be a preferred supplier.
   - Our standard for the number of parts per assembly is 63. Unless you can reduce your current 128 parts for each assembly, you cannot be a preferred supplier.

Norming Your Capacity to Add Value

Whereas Tier 1 businesses focus on their customers, Tier 2s spend most of their time trading market shares with each other. In the workstation market, Hewlett-Packard, number two behind Sun Microsystems, offers 20 percent discounts to Sun users who switch to HP. Sun makes the same offer to HP users.

According to Michael Porter, a spokesman for Tier 2 management, "The essence of strategy formulation is coping with competition." The customer is an afterthought. Tier 1's management mindset shows the difference between the tiers. It may be summarized this way: "The essence of strategy formulation is helping customers cope with their competition—internal competition from operating costs and external competition from rival market penetrators."

Tier 1 customer-clients never see products or services. They see only surrogates of their ability to contribute to customer value. These surrogates are presented to them by their comanagers in the form of *norms,* averages of the comanagers' ability to integrate products and related services into systems and apply them to improve customer operations.

Norms are representations of value-adding outcomes. But they possess a greater reality than the products and services and systems whose contributions they represent. Because they are in dollar amounts, norms enable a customer to hurdle the product phase of getting to value and get right into the value phase itself.

Tier 1 comanagers are merchants of their norms. They paper their customer markets with them, posting them everywhere as SalesWorld 2000 versions of product announcements. In a sense, that is what they are: advertisements for their "products," which are outcomes rather than means of achieving them.

As a result of showing and telling their norms, Tier 1 comanagers wage norm wars. Their targets are not rival Tier 1s but customer managers whose performance a comanager can improve. Comanagers are engaged and disengaged on the basis of their norms. Norm leaders get into partnerships by flashing their norms and backing them up with value propositions that prove how the norms can be more closely approached. Losers in the norm wars take their outmoded norms back to the drawing boards. While they are working on rejuvenating them, they are missing out on the experience of learning how to apply them for even higher proficiency. Going back to the shop for repairs can be the beginning of a death spiral.

Norms are a comanager's resume. When he plays his norm card—or speaks his N-number (for norm)—he is challenging customer managers to take him on.

Norms are of, by, and for customer operations. They focus the comanager-customer manager dialog on the customer's business where it belongs. At the same time, they prevent the customer from getting into the comanager's business in the manner of a purchasing agent, where he would X-ray the comanager's product specifications or measure the statute miles between his plants and the comanager's warehouses. Instead, norm challenges open the door for the comanager to move into the customer's operations wherever the comanager's norms apply. Acting as credentials, his norms give him entry.

A comanager's norm challenge to reduce downtime costs propels him into a customer's manufacturing operations to see if and how he can bring the customer manager new profits.

A comanager's norm challenge to eliminate scrap and re-work propels him into the customer's manufacturing operations for additional profit-improvement opportunities.

No customer manager asks, What are you trying to sell? No comanager asks, Where can I find leads and someone to sell to? Products as units of sale are as dead as sales strategy itself. Norming is about advantaging. Comanagers ask, Can coming closer to my norms advantage you? When a customer manager suspects that the answer may be yes, he or she asks in return, How can you get me there?

Tier 1s rise and fall on the value of their norms. So do their individual comanagers. If either of them fails to keep ahead of their customers in being able to get the most value out of customer operations with the most efficient levels of investment, they will be tripped up by their norms. In a single glance, their applications skills and process smarts will be revealed. Stripped of the twin "osities" of vendor selling—pomposity that you are the best and verbosity in proclaiming it—you will be naked to your norms.

Acquiring the Tier 1 Mindset

Tier 1 comes as close as possible to being a knowledge business, the kind of intelligent organization that uses its brain power to manufacture solutions rather than products and applies its solutions to customer operations rather than its own. It is no different than other businesses in the fact that it manages know-how. Its differentiation comes from the type of know-how it manages, which is based on applications, and its dedication to managing it for the continuous improvement of its customers' competitiveness.

Tier 1 businesses are often called "mind shops" because they outsource support functions, ally with multiple contract suppliers, create virtual organization formats that come together and break apart on a project basis, and minimally define their core capabilities as the men and women who can comanage their customers' operations. In pre-SalesWorld 2000 terms, Tier 1s "sell" one thing: not knowledge, but the improved outcomes that their customer-clients can realize when they apply a Tier 1's comanagement knowledge.

If you want to achieve Tier 1 status, you must be able to comanage the continuous profit improvement of a customer processing operation or product category or at least a major component of a customer facility. The value chain to "get to Tier 1" goes like this:

- If you make speedometers for automobile manufacturers, you are a Tier 2.
- If you become a systems integrator by assembling dashboards out of your speedometers and other suppliers' oil pressure gauges, gas gauges, temperature gauges, and clocks, you are still a Tier 2.
- If you comanage an automobile manufacturer's dashboard assembly line to re-engineer its work flow and reduce its cycle times in addition to acting as an outsource of integrated dashboard systems, you may become a Tier 1. It depends on the value you add to your customer's outcomes: how much you help increase his productivity and cash flow and how much you help reduce his costs of manufacturing each car.

Tier 2s that seek a shortcut to getting to Tier 1 by creating or acquiring consulting organizations fall into two traps. They try to sell consulting services as if they were just another product line, pricing them at an hourly rate.

When consultation is packaged like a product and offered at a price, it becomes a commodity. Figure 3-2 shows what commodity consulting services look like when they are promoted by

Figure 3-2. Hourly rate card models.

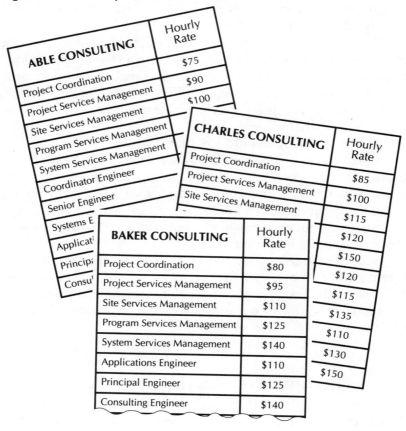

a price list in the form of hourly rate cards. Like product prices, the hourly rates on each card are cost-based and influenced by competition. They have no relationship whatsoever to value. As a result, hourly rates are invitations to be discounted. The consultants they rate have been converted from intellectual capitalists into undifferentiated vendors.

The second trap that Tier 2s fall into is to use consultation as a loss leader to sell their products. They fail to recognize that any kind of selling, whether it is selling consultation or using consultation to sell products, is Tier 2. Tier 2 consultancies risk being flawed by the perception that their recommendations are self-serving smokescreens for product sales rather than client-serving. But being a service division of a manufacturer brings with it an even more corrosive bias—the bias of a hardware-dominated product mentality.

You can see the unregenerate vendor mindset at work in the case of the industrial packager who sets up a Display Consulting Business to sell 10 percent of its brown-box cardboard, a commodity, at value-added margins. The consulting business is looked at as an upscale strategy to circumvent the "curse of commodity cardboard."

A Tier 1 mindset would say that in-store display is a revenue-based sales promotion business, not a cardboard-based marketing business. Its market is not purchasing agents who buy cardboard but brand, product, and sales managers who rely on in-store point-of-purchase displays to add value to their sales mix. Sales promotion consultants, not cardboard sales representatives, should be its "point people."

Instead of knowing how to justify cardboard costs, the consultancy must know how to comanage a total sales campaign that mixes sales promotion with national media and co-op store advertising in order to serve direct profit-per-product business objectives.

Becoming a General Contractor

The customers who become Tier 1 clients position Tier 1 as their general contractors to take three major processes out of their hands and off their books:

1. Their *acquisition processes*, such as vendor screening and selection, quality control, inventory management, and price negotiation
2. Their *implementation processes*, such as integrating vendor products and services into systems and re-engineering the customer processes they drive
3. Their *management processes*, such as comanaging profit improvement projects by insourcing or outsourcing customer business categories or operating facilities

Drug companies call their strategy to take over patient care "disease management," targeting major chronic diseases like asthma, diabetes, ulcers, epilepsy, and depression. By comanaging total patient care instead of just supplying the drug components of a care system, drug companies put themselves in position to help reduce hospital costs by practicing preventive medicine. As hospital bills come down under disease management, the drug companies gainshare in the savings.

Health maintenance organizations (HMOs) are the drug companies' natural partners. Their alliances are based on the common objective of keeping patients from having to be admitted to hospital care or, after discharge, to be readmitted. Outpatient treatment with drugs saves money for HMOs and makes money for the drug companies.

In some partnerships, drug companies act as multivendor distributors. Eli Lilly manages antibiotic programs that offer a mix of Lilly and non-Lilly drugs. Medco provides disease management for diabetic patients even though it does not make insulin.

- Philip Morris is the Tier 1 comanager of the cigarette category for its supermarket clients. In partnership with each chain's category managers, Philip Morris plans continuous improvement of the category's profit contribution. The single best planogram they agree on contains the optimal mix of Philip Morris and other brands that can generate maximum earnings from the category. In one profit improvement project after another, a Philip Morris comanager and client manager mix and match packing, stocking, and shelving options like these:
  —Optimal brand mix per carton and per pack
  —Optimal sales per brand per square foot
  —Optimal margin per brand
  —Optimal turnover per brand
  —Optimal inventory and minimal acceptable stockout per brand

How does Philip Morris get to become the general contractor for Acme Supermarkets' cigarette category? Instead of trying to sell Acme on stocking and shelving more Philip Morris brands to the exclusion of competitors, Philip Morris counsels Acme on continuously improving cigarette category profits. In this way, Philip Morris acts as a market expander.

- EDS (Electronic Data Systems) is the Tier 1 comanager of Chicago's parking ticket collections. In partnership with the city's collections manager, EDS plans continuous improvement in total uncollected tickets outstanding. In one profit improvement project after another, an EDS comanager and client manager create a continuous recovery process based on criteria like these:
  —Optimal dollars collected per dollars invested
  —Optimal dollars per collection
  —Optimal dollars collected per each 30 days

How does EDS get to become the general contractor for Chicago's parking ticket collections? Instead of selling the city on an EDS-prescribed system of relational database software and computer workstation platforms to the exclusion of competitive systems, EDS counsels Chicago on continuously improving parking revenues. In this way, EDS acts as a supplemental legislative funder.

Maintaining Standards Leadership

Oligopoly characterizes Tier 1 control of almost every major industry. Two Tier 1s, three at most, can serve the major needs of the 20 percent or so of an industry's clients who account for 80 percent or so of its business. Over time, few industries will need even the third major Tier 1, which will fall out as the result of ineffective management of its revenue-producing intellectual assets or the costs of its goods acquisition processes from Tier 2.

As a result of mergers and acquisitions of duplicative capabilities, a small number of Tier 1s are coming to dominate each industry. Other, less formal consolidations are occurring as alliances. In many cases, alliances are virtual businesses in and of themselves. Some are transient, existing only for a specific project or to devise a specific process or product. Others last longer, such as allied businesses that agree to serve a common market with shared technologies, conduct pure research that no one of them alone can afford, or use concentrated purchasing power to negotiate backbreaker deals with Tier 2 suppliers.

Becoming an oligarch, which ensures survival as a Tier 1, means owning the standard performance for adding value in a major category of your customers' businesses. Since no organization can be the standard bearer of value in more than a few categories, becoming an "alpha Tier 1" is a process of creative destruction.

You start at the top by touching the customer, where you can look back down the value chain and ask yourself, "How little do I need to own?" in order to command continuous touch.

By creatively destroying the need to own low-end values, you come as close as you can to an ideal configuration for a Tier 1 business. There are two rules to follow:

1. Never manufacture anything you can buy, rent, lease, or joint-venture.
2. Never buy anything you can rent or lease.

A Tier 1 business remains a Tier 1 only as long as its standards represent leadership performance as an improver of its customer-clients' operations. Standards leadership is the compelling reason for a Tier 1's acceptance as comanager—what else does a customer need a comanager for except to bring him or her closer to more competitive performance?

A Tier 1's mission must always be standards-specific: to bring continuous improvement to each customer's current standards of performance so that Tier 1's own track record of standard outcomes is continuously improved. Relaxation in standards growth can be hazardous to Tier 1 health.

Standards building requires that a Tier 1 conduct business according to five guidelines:

1. A common understanding that standards building is everybody's job number one
2. A combative attitude to waging standards warfare

3. A healthy respect for measuring standard values
4. A proud publicizing of superior standards
5. A fierce dedication to standards leadership

The larger a Tier 1, the more vulnerable it is to standards competition from small specialist Tier 1s. Large organizations must decentralize into federations of autonomous specialist businesses in order to be able to go head to head with niche competitors. At the niche level, businesses are already autonomous and specialist and can become "virtually large" at will by putting together strategic alliances of extended capabilities— allies who are themselves autonomous and specialist and who hold standards leadership in their individual specialties.

Big Tier 1s must get out of their own way both operationally and psychologically. "Size arrogance" often afflicts them. Jack Welch, chairman of General Electric, exemplifies the "ancient paradigm" of large company blindsidedness when he says that "The only reason people are small is that they can't get big." A more appropriate mindset for leadership in SalesWorld 2000 is to say that the only way to capitalize on bigness as far as comanagement is concerned is to break up into a lot of smallnesses. Nobody benefits from bigness itself. The objective is to know everything you need to know about a customer's key performance indicators and how to make continuous improvements in them. However big you have to be to do that better than anyone else is as big or as small as you need to be.

Sourcing Consultative Comanagers

What is consulting? It is *the improvement of a client manager's contribution to profits.* Consulting is defined by its result, not by the steps in its process, because a consultant's client is funded according to results. In turn, the consultant is funded according to his contribution to client results. If results fail to create positive value, the answer to the question, "What kind of consultant is he or she?" is *none.*

With similar pragmatism, the consultant's client is not

going to remain a manager for long without positive results to show from his or her investments in a comanager's consultation. Consultants are not judged by the quantity or quality of their counsel. Nor do they earn their keep by being timely or innovative. They are evaluated by the return they contribute on their clients' investments.

A positive ROI attests that a comanager has consulted; he or she has added a greater value than its cost. Even though the comanager may have done everything according to the book— listened carefully and then used prudence to advise, documentation to recommend, and compassion to compromise—a negative or low ROI makes out the consultant to be an added and unreclaimed cost.

In and of itself, consulting is the way a comanager does business, not as an offering but as a business style that positions him side by side with a customer manager in the posture of partnership, not confrontationally eyeball to eyeball across a barrier desk. A comanager knows that as soon as he can see a customer's eyeballs, he has stopped consulting with his partner and has begun to confront an adversary.

Figure 3-3 shows the two sourcing options for comanagers.

Option 1: You can upgrade the convertible 20 to 30 percent of your traditional sales force to become value-adding sellers by training them to apply Mack Hanan's Consultative Selling™* strategies for your products and services to the customer operations they sell into.

Option 2. You can recruit a current line of business managers or business function managers from your customers' industries and train them to apply Consultative Selling™ strategies for your products and services to the operations they are already experienced in managing. They bring with them a knowledge of a client manager's key performance indicators, a database of client operating norms, and best industry practices.

*For a fuller discussion of consultative practice management, see Mack Hanan, *Consultative Selling™*, 5th edition, AMACOM, 1995. Comanagement is the logical extension of Consultative Selling.

Figure 3-3. Comanager sourcing options.

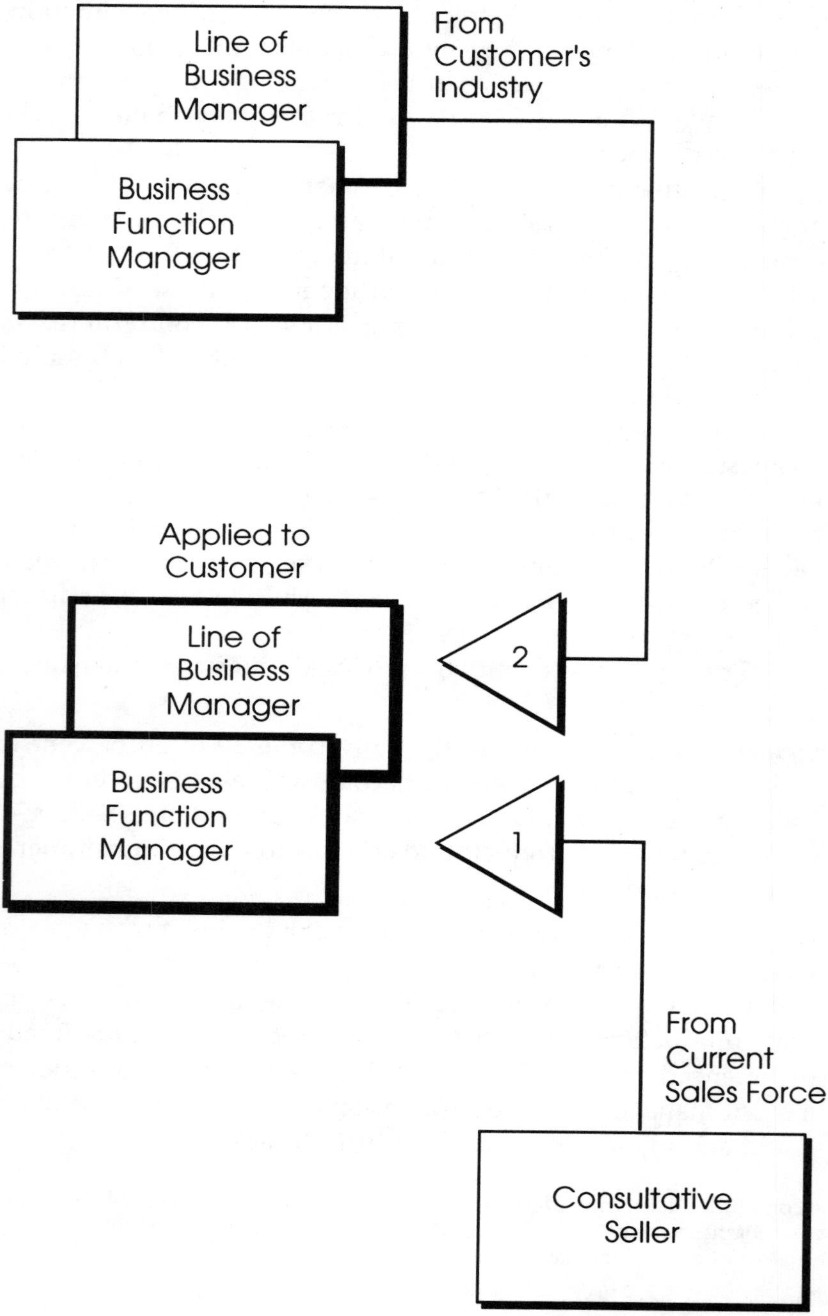

If you choose Option 1, your comanagers have a head start in applications knowledge about your products and services. They must be trained in everything else. Option 2 reverses the tradeoff. Your comanagers have a head start in everything except applications knowledge and managing a consultative practice, in both of which they must be trained.

Becoming preoccupied with your comanagers, their sourcing, and resourcing is a priority for every company's top managers. Along with selecting their own managers, nothing is more important than ensuring the topnotch quality of the comanagers they send out to partner with key customer-clients and applying the same rigorous standards to the comanagers furnished by their suppliers that they let in.

Comanagement is the critical success factor of SalesWorld 2000 because it is the last bastion of human intervention in business-to-business relationships. The SalesWorld market is for people, not products. Although Tier 1 providers will still go on providing goods and services, their single most critical category of supply will be their comanagers. Tier 1s will be known by the stock-on-hand of best-practicing comanagers they can deliver just-in-time, install in customer operations, service, and maintain. Their comanagers will be more important than their products, which, as commodities, can be obtained anywhere in the Tier 2 universe.

A best-practicing comanager, branded by the possession of industry-standard norms, represents the only competitive uniqueness remaining in business that can compel customers to go after it and insist on acquiring at the equivalent of a premium price. Customers will be looking for the indispensable "nose for profits" of a Clark Gable who saw the value of playing Rhett Butler in *Gone With the Wind* in contrast to a Gary Cooper who was pleased that it would be Gable "who's falling flat on his face and not Gary Cooper," or of a Steve Wozniak whose invention became the foundation of Apple Computer in contrast to his employers at Hewlett-Packard whose debating teams turned him down at one wedding-cake layer of management after the other.

Yet in spite of Tier 1's emphasis on human added values, some aspects of intellectual capital are being replaced by knowledge-worker-type software for the same reasons of cost and efficiency that physical capital is being automated by Tier 2. The diagnosis of customer problems and the prescription of optimal solutions, two of a Tier 1's key areas of expertise, are being executed by expert systems instead of experts themselves. This moves the premium on human capital even further up the value chain, away from problem definition and solution prescription to managing maximum outcomes. Tier 1 comanagers have their diagnostic and prescriptive "consultants on a chip" to support them, freeing them from doing the work themselves, so that they can focus on the role that gives them the greatest payout and, with gainsharing, the greatest payback.

Partnering "Them" and "Us"

Customer-focus, customer-orientation, customer-intimacy, being customer-driven, and getting close to the customer are the epitaphs of Tier 2 businesses that passed the 1980s talking a good game that they could never play. The more they publicized their alleged market drive, the more focused they turned out to be on their own businesses: empowering their own people instead of their customers, improving their own products instead of their customers' operations, and creating technology instead of applying it.

For every business that brought its customers into residence within its R&D, manufacturing, or sales operations, making them its partners in achieving customer satisfaction from the inception, hundreds of others made customer satisfaction a postlude, not prelude, to their decisions.

The fact of the matter turned out to be that customer orientation can never be accomplished operationally. Unless a way can be found to couple suppliers and their customers organizationally so that they work *with* each other as well as *for* each other, customers will remain "them" and suppliers will remain "us" or the other way around.

Comanagement strategy eliminates them-us. It brings together consultative comanagers and their customer-clients in miniorganizations structured as Joint Profit Projects, or "JP

Squares." Each JPP is a virtual business. It develops its own profit-improvement plan, sets mutual profit-contributing objectives, and generates a steady state of profit projects to realize them. The "products" of each project are dollars.

Comanaged JPPs are customer-oriented by design because customers are designed into them. They solve the main problem of customer-orientation, which is working in separate spaces. Comanagers and their customer counterparts share real space and cyberspace twenty-four hours, seven days a week. They are always accessible to each other. Their shared databases are equally accessible, providing the only operational boundaries to their work. *Managers with equal access to the same data are equal to each other*, so there are no hierarchical boundaries either. Everyone is "us." No one is "them," outsiders or interlopers. With this joint insider relationship, the parties all work for the same boss—either a customer line-of-business manager and, through him, his customers in the external marketplace—or a customer business function manager and, through him, the line-of-business managers who are his internal customers. Directly or indirectly, a comanager's "boss of bosses" is always a manager of cash inflows.

Even though they are not generally incorporated, JPPs led in tandem by a supplier comanager and a customer manager take on their own corporate identity. They have team spirit, with much the same motivation as entrepreneurs when they gainshare in their results. They also share the entrepreneurial sense of mortality called "shortgevity," which reminds them that they are only as good—and as permanent—as their standards of performance. This incents them to manage each virtual business like they own it.*

No traditional supplier relationship, no matter how intimate it professes to be or how relationship-managed, can approximate the conjugal partnership of a comanaged JPP. Shared objectives bond the teammates. Shared risk and reward motivate them to take care of each other; no one is easily expendable or, like a vendor, an alternate source that is instantly replicable.

*For a fuller discussion of self-empowered management strategies, see Mack Hanan, *Manage Like You Own It*, AMACOM, 1994.

Within a Joint Profit Project, no sales calls are made. No third-party coaches are required to intermediate with alleged power sources or influentials. No communications gaps allow things to fall through the cracks. Along the lines of the Entenmann brothers model for running a business, the principals are always talking openly, hearing and overhearing each other so that nobody misses anything. Their orientation is preordained by their proximity; comanagers face up to customer needs because they face their customer managers every waking minute.

When General Foods undertook due diligence on Entenmann, prior to acquiring the regional baker, the diligencers were duly appalled to discover that such a high-growth, high-velocity market-penetrating business was being run by a team of brothers sitting desk-by-desk in an open, no-frills office above a bakery. They spent all their time on the telephone talking to customers and face to face talking to each other. "How do you guys make any money this way?" the GFers asked.

"This way," the Entenmann brothers answered, speaking in the same way that they worked—together.

Planning Your Kind of Tier 1

If you want to manage your business as a Tier 1, there are half a dozen decisions you are going to have to make to test how feasible it is for you to be primarily or exclusively an intellectual capital provider. Before you get to your options, you start out with three givens:

1. You must have a Consultative Selling™ force of profit project managers to comanage your customer clients.
2. You must have an acquisition process that allows automated outsourcing from Tier 2 suppliers on behalf of your comanaged customer-clients.
3. You must have an information function that maintains your databases on customer operations.

Here are your six categories of options:

1. What will our vision be?
   - What differentiating business positions will be available to us?

- How much revenue and share of market will each position gain for us? How much profit? How much return on investment?
- What critical success factors will each position require? What will they add up to as the cost of our asset base?
- What fit with what customers in what markets will each position enable us to make?

2. What management structure must support each vision?
   - What organization models are available to us?
   - How does each model contribute to maximizing profitable revenues and minimizing costs?
   - How is the customer built into each model?
   - What type of leadership does each model require?
   - What type of capability base does each model require? What mix of internal and virtual assets is necessary? What is total capability cost?

3. What market segments will we own?
   - What markets are available to us with each capability base?
   - How much profitable revenue and share of market can we expect from each? At how much cost?
   - Within each market, what business lines and business functions will be our customers?
   - Who will be our competitors for each business line and business function? What is the core business position of each competitor? With what capability base? Derived from what technologies and applications expertise?
   - How much improved profits can we expect to add to each market? At how much return to us on our investment? At how much return on each customer's investment with us?

4. Who will our preferred suppliers be?
   - What sources are available to us for each market segment?
   - How much will it cost to do business with each source?

5. What will constrain us?
   - What uncontrollable critical success factors can cause significant deviations from our planned growth?

- What is the potential cost of each constraint?
6. All things considered, what is our most likely 3–5 year Pro Forma?
    - What are the most likely amounts of sources and distribution of funds for the 20 percent in each category that will contribute up to 80 percent?
    - What is our worst case scenario for a viable business?

Of the three types of management style—by anticipation, reaction, or crisis—only the first two can keep you in business as a Tier 1. Managers who are good at anticipating change and convincing in communicating their foresight can be first to market with incremental changes that can be easily absorbed by their customer-clients. Close behind them are the secondary Tier 1s who react to the leaders. Crisis managers who react too far behind the curve and then try to do everything at once are candidates for acquisition by the anticipators and reactors.

Part II

Capitalizing on the Shocks

How to Own Account Control as Your Customers' Comanager

4

Proposal Shock: The End of Bids

Comanagement transforms a supplier. He graduates from purveying products, services, or systems to being a provider of funds. The funds take the form of the incremental profits that the applications of the comanager's systems of products and services can contribute.

A comanager's proposals undergo a similar transformation. Bids are ended. Instead, comanagers propose the multiplication of a customer-client's money by investing it in profit projects that are run under a Tier 1's comanagement with a customer manager. If you are a Tier 1, each proposal is a quid pro quo: If the customer-client will let you borrow some of his funds as if they were a short-term loan, you will return more than one dollar for each dollar you borrow. The interest on the loan—the value you add to each dollar—is the customer-client's improved profit. It can come from three sources:

1. New revenues from increased turnover
2. Increased margins on current revenues
3. Reduced or eliminated costs

New revenues may come from opening up new markets or enlarging a customer-client's penetration of existing markets so that inventory and receivables turn over faster. Increased margins may come from adding value to a customer's products or services and their resulting value-based pricing. Reduced or eliminated costs can come from rationalized or restructured operations.

As a Tier 1, each profit proposal you make rests on a similar assumption about each dollar of customer funds you request: it is always going to realize optimal multiplication under your comanagement, which assumes prudent risk:

- If you are proposing to increase customer revenues, the revenues will represent the optimal improvement over current revenues that can be generated by the proposed investment.
- If you are proposing to reduce customer costs, the savings will represent the optimal reduction of current costs that can be subtracted by the proposed investment.

Sometimes you can streamline a customer-client's work flows. Other times you can shorten his cycle times, reduce or eliminate his nonvalue-adding costs, improve his productivity, or you can propose to manage one of his operations with improved cost-effectiveness. The more ways you can multiply his funds, the more valuable you can be to him as a comanager.

Seeing Unseen Opportunities

The sale as the basic unit of transaction has been replaced by a comanager's profit projects. A JPP always has the objective of improving the outcome of a customer's operation. Products and services that support the project, together with teams of intellectual capitalists who apply them in the most cost-effective manner, are contracted for on a project-specific basis by its comanager. When one project ends, another team and its resource package begins the next attempt to improve the outcome even more or improve another contributor to customer competitiveness.

In this way, a comanager becomes his customer's outsource of improved contributions to corporate profits. Continuous improvement requires a steady state of profit projects that no customer can manage alone. A single unsuccessful project can kill this continuity. So can downtime between projects, which keeps the capital invested in a customer's operation from circulating and his sales from turning over.

A customer who owns best practices today can find himself brought back down to the industry average tomorrow. His own customers' satisfaction with him can never be bought, only rented. "Sustainable competitive advantage" in SalesWorld 2000 is an oxymoron. Any advantage that could be sustainable would not be competitive; it would be monopolistic. If competitive, it could not be sustainable; it would be up for grabs.

Nevertheless, no customer-client can have a good year this year and a bad year next year and still have a job the third year. Reliability—being "on plan" by meeting his key performance indicators—must be every manager's middle name. For line of business managers, reliability means continually making more money from every dollar invested to fund their operations. For business function managers, reliability means continually reducing the cost required by each line of business manager to make each dollar.

Comanagers must be reliable seers of opportunities to improve profits that their customer managers do not see; or they must be able to see opportunities from afar when they are still nascent and no one else is yet competing to fund them; or they must be able to see bigger opportunities that a smaller opportunity may be only a part of; or they must see alternate ways to make a proposal fundable or manageable or how to migrate one opportunity into another and to combine projects to reduce their cumulative costs or to increase their total outcome.

These are the ways that comanagers add value to customer managers and, in the process, make themselves invaluable.

Becoming a Source of Cash Flows

Proposing as a comanager positions you as the sole responsible source of the cash flows that you promise to deliver. You become their dedicated supplier. Your comanagement of the continuous improvement of a customer-client's competitiveness depends on the continuity with which you pay off on each proposal. Your proposals, not your products, become your high-margin money-makers because they are the high-value adders to your customers. Their money values earn margins that the performance values of your products cannot approximate.

Profit proposals are the comanager's version of products. Comanagers think of themselves as being in the business of manufacturing the profits that they propose. They apply familiar criteria of manufacturing management to proposal development, production, quality control, inventory, and delivery:

- High proposal quality   = minimum defects
- Low proposal reject rate   = minimum scrap
- Low proposal return rate   = minimum repairs
- High proposal productivity   = minimum downtime
- Low proposal unit cost   = minimum resources
- Just-in-time proposal delivery = minimum inventory

A comanager's profit proposal and a customer manager's business case are identical twins, based on the same rationale that top management will get back more money than it hands out by funding the proposal. In both cases, the costs and benefits are expressed in terms of streams of cash inflows and outflows.* Figure 4-1 shows a model format for analyzing a proposal's benefits and their costs.

Top management should have no way to tell who has originated a profit project, as in the following proposal, where it is impossible to tell whether the originator is a customer's own chief information officer (CIO) or his comanager:

What if we can help reach the corporate objective 90 days sooner to finance the opening of one hundred new stores in the next twelve months?

We propose to do this by enabling each existing store to contribute an additional $200,000 to this year's profits. Approximately $150,000 will come from costs saved by computerizing their checkout stations. The

*For a fuller discussion of a customer manager's funding process, see Mack Hanan, *Consultative Budgeting,* AMACOM, 1994.

Figure 4-1. Cost-benefit analysis.

INVESTMENT	Y0	Y1	Y2	Y3
1				
2				
3				
4				
5 TOTAL CASH OUT				

CONTRIBUTION FROM SALES	Y1	Y2	Y3
6 Increased revenues			
7 less increased costs of sales			
8 NET CASH IN (6 − 7)			

CONTRIBUTION FROM REDUCED COSTS	Y1	Y2	Y3
9 Fixed costs:			
10 Variable costs:			
11 NET CASH IN (9 + 10)			

NET CASH FLOWS	Y0	Y1	Y2	Y3
12 Cash flow [(8 + 11) − 5]				
13 Cumulative cash flow				

remaining $50,000 will come from eliminating the cost of correcting checker errors. The total annual savings equal an average week's gross sales for the top 20 percent of our stores, the equivalent of making this year fifty-three weeks long.

The "sales negotiations" about profit proposals take place over the costs and benefits of cost-benefit analysis, not product prices or performance. Typical negotiating points include issues like these:

- What if we reduce the investment—do the cash flow benefits decrease proportionately?
- What if we spread out the investment—how much sooner can we get to payback of the initial funds?
- What if we try to gain a revenue effect as well as cost savings so that our rate of return is increased—what added sales can be generated by reducing downtime?

Presuming a Call on Funds

A comanager's proposal strategy follows a six-step sequence. This is how his thought process works:

1. *How does my focus fit the customer's business strategy?*
I focus on improving the profit contributions of some of the critical success factors in one or more of a customer-client's profit-centered lines of business or cost-centered business functions. Which of their competitive advantages that I can improve fits with an objective in the customer's overall business strategy? Because customers put their funds where their objectives are, I need to make my proposal an enabler of a business goal so that it will be a priority for investment.

2. *What am I going to compete against?*
One or more of the critical success factors that I focus on are currently making competitively disadvantageous contributions to the customer-client's profits. Some are contributing unnecessary or excess costs. Others are contributing insufficient or undependable revenues or margins. Which of them—costs, revenues, margins, or all three—should I propose to compete against?

3. *What is the minimum improvement I can prescribe?*
The customer-client has established hurdle rates for the minimum value he or she will accept from an investment and from an investment's rate of return. By how little can I exceed customer minimums and still be compelling? By adhering to a policy of making minimal improvements, I can reduce his investment and the time it takes to pay it back and thereby minimize the customer-client's risk in going ahead with me.

4. *What is my optimal solution to deliver the minimum improvement?*
What is my single best solution to improve the customer-client's advantage, as defined by the ratio between each dollar's worth of effectiveness that comes out of the solution compared to each dollar's worth of cost that must go into it?*

5. *What will make my proposal closable?*
What is the optimal funding strategy that will ensure the customer-client's sponsorship in supporting my proposal?

6. *How do I follow up?*
What should my migration strategy be so that I can keep on earning my right to comanage by providing continuous improvement?

Proposing to Improve KPIs

Every critical success factor in a line of business or business function that you propose to comanage already has a customer manager who is trying to realize its objectives. His or her performance is compared against objectives by measurements that are known as key performance indicators, or KPIs.

Some KPIs measure a manager's operating performance. Other KPIs measure financial performance. Wherever they lag against objectives, KPIs become a comanager's proposal targets. A comanager can make three types of proposals to bring improvement to a customer's manager's performance:

1. Prevent a manager from deviating from a KPI, keeping him on plan.
2. Correct a deviation from a KPI, bringing him back on plan.
3. Exceed a KPI, helping him to do better than 100 percent of plan.

As a result, comanagers' profit proposals make them surrogates of their customer managers. Unlike product and service

*For a fuller discussion of value-based proposing, see Mack Hanan, *Competing on Value*, with Peter Karp, AMACOM, 1991.

vendors, comanagers never propose something like 98 percent on-time delivery for themselves; they propose it for a customer manager for whom it is a KPI. The comanager's added value might come from helping a customer maintain his current on-time performance at the 98 percent level or raising it to 99 percent if it is competitively advantageous for the customer to do so.

A comanager's ability to measure the improved impacts of profit proposals on customer KPIs is every bit as important as the ability to propose their improvement. An unmeasured improvement, which means that it cannot be quantified, is no improvement. Two types of measurement skill are crucial. One is knowing how a customer manager's performance is currently being measured. The other is knowing how to measure the value you add to his performance by the improvements that you propose.

Your value added—*VAdd* for short—can be measured in three ways:

1. How much total value you add to a customer's performance as a profit contributor
2. How soon you add your value
3. How cost-effectively you add your value as calculated by dividing the VAdd the customer realizes by his or her cost to realize it

The VAdd process is shown in Figure 4-2. It starts with measuring the customer-client's current performance and using it as your benchmark. The next step is the customer's investment to improve on current performance. This incurs a negative value that must be regained, which occurs in the third step when the investment is repaid. The customer is free from risk. In the last step, the customer realizes the benefits from investment that allow him to perform with added value.

Approaching Zero Risk

In SalesWorld 2000, value must be added or funds will be denied. If they are going to stay competitive, customers must get

Figure 4-2. The VAdd process.

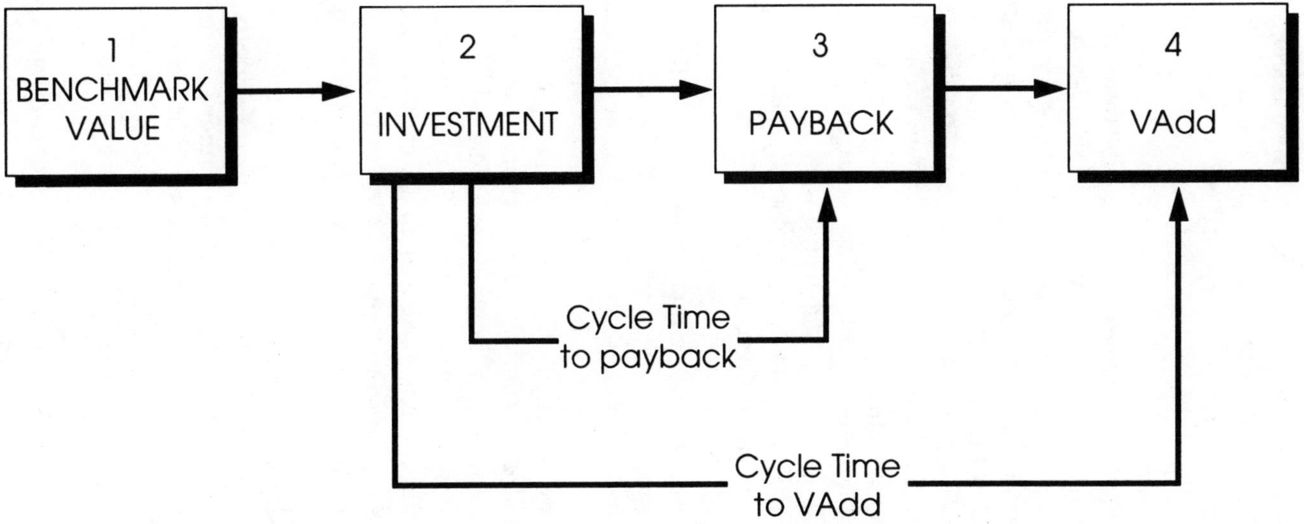

the greatest possible value out of every dollar they fund, they must get their value as soon as possible after they commit their funds, and they must get the full value they pay for at the exact time they expect it.

Risk in getting an investment paid back or making the proposed amount of money on it has become unacceptable. Customers have always attempted to minimize uncertainty by taking chances only in small bites where the probability of loss can be minimized and the severity of its impact carefully controlled. This allows them to think of it as a "calculated risk." Calculation of a risk is a chancy proposition because investments must be made based on what is known today whereas their returns can be realized only in the unknown future.

A comanager's profit proposals cannot be chancy propositions. They must approach a customer-client's need for zero risk. Zero risk is based on three constraints that must be built into each comanagement proposal:

1. *Cost certainty*, which guarantees that the customer's investment is *"the* investment, the *whole* investment, and *nothing but* the investment," so help the comanager, and that it will not be exceeded by continuing requests for more funds

2. *Payback certainty*, which guarantees the time when the customer will be made whole again, releasing him from the risk of not regaining his investment

3. *Outcome certainty*, which guarantees realization of the total proposed value of the benefits so that the expected return on the customer's investments can be ensured

Zero-risk criteria for investing funds steer customers to favor comanaging certain types of costs over others. Investments to upgrade existing plant and equipment, to make innovations incrementally through continuous improvements rather than attempt blockbuster-type breakthroughs, and to improve core capabilities instead of diversifying are on most approval lists for risk control.

Comanagement proposals must acknowledge the unaffordability of customer risk. If a comanager's cost-benefit analysis could speak for him, it would sound like this to a customer: "For every $1.00 with which you fund me, you will receive $1.50, for a 50 cent increment. Your original investment will be paid back within ninety days. Over the first three years, your total net pre-tax gain will be $500,000."

An investment's performance according to plan is a far more serious proposition than the performance of a product, service, or system. Nonperforming or underperforming funds create two kinds of losses. One is their direct cost, which may be reclaimable. The other is their opportunity cost, which is lost forever. No one can recapture the opportunity to have invested the same funds at a better rate of return. For the comanager who incurs serious opportunity costs for a customer, partnership may be a nonsustainable experience.

5

Data Shock: The End of Unproposable Information

A comanager's position description is based on a single core concept: *continuous customer improvement*. This is a databased job specification, so dependent on data that comanagement and data management are one and the same.

Data meet three requirements for comanagers:

- Data are required to benchmark the key indicators of a customer manager's performance in order to target leads for profit projects.
- Data are required to measure periodic progress on a milestone-by-milestone basis toward the proposed outcome of each profit project.
- Data are required to calculate the cost-effectiveness of each improved outcome by measuring how soon each dollar a customer invests is paid back and how much interest he or she earns on it in the form of positive cash flow.

These three categories of data are *proposal-critical* because they are necessary for targeting proposable leads and prescribing closable profit projects. SalesWorld 2000 marks the end of irrelevant data, which are data that are in the interesting-but-unproposable category, not worth the labor cost of collection, access, and assessment.

The collection of unproposable data has become a cottage

industry in Tier 2, where it masquerades as "research." It is often listed as if data were laundry, with the same useless but cosmic inquiries appearing again and again:

- What is the customer's corporate culture?
- What is the philosophy of the organization?
- What are the major concerns the company is facing, such as competition or the economy?
- Where do you see the business in the future, both in the short term and the long term?
- How will the business be different five years from today?
- How realistic are the company's goals?

If the answers are not known or cannot easily be concocted, the research purveyors suggest a scripted "request for a research meeting" that goes like this:

> Hello. I've sensed a fit between our products and your company, so over the past few weeks I've done a little homework. I wonder if you could spare thirty or forty minutes to meet with me so that I can confirm my understanding of your business, the possible fit for our products, and the names of a few others in the organization.

This confession of ignorance based on *sensing* a fit and doing a *little* homework has an incredible objective: "To present ourselves as a credible resource."

If you hold yourself out as a comanager, you permit the inference that you are expert in maximizing outcomes from applying the solutions you provide. Your outcomes are your products. But the data that support your expertise enable you to commercialize them.

- If your expertise is the reduction of direct labor costs, you must own a database containing your norms for the maximum acceptable amount of direct labor content that can be applied to an operation so that you can use your norms to screen a customer's actuals.

You must also own databases containing your norms for the maximum acceptable amount of manhours that can be charged to sorting materials, tool adjustment, setup costs as a percent of production hours, and overtime for finished-goods inspection.

▪ If your expertise is in the reduction of indirect labor costs, you must own a database containing your norms for the maximum acceptable amount of indirect labor content that can be applied to materials handling, production scheduling, layout inspection, machine repair, and maintenance so that you can use your norms to screen a customer's actuals.

▪ If your expertise is the reduction of scrap costs, you must own a database containing your norms for the maximum acceptable amount of manhours that can be applied to salvage, sorting, and materials handling; remanufacturing; and unproductive direct labor so that you can use your norms to screen a customer's actuals.

▪ If your expertise is in the reduction of inventory costs, you must own a database containing your norms for the maximum acceptable amount of manhours that can be applied to materials building per inventory turn along with the minimum acceptable number of turns so that you can use your norms to screen a customer's actuals.

This is what proposable data look like in SalesWorld 2000, the polar opposite of a vendor sales representative's blue-sheet data on "how well your base is covered with each buying influence" and where your place is in the "sales funnel."

Databasing the Proposal Process

If you are a Tier 1, client-customers ask two questions when you propose to be their comanager:

▪ How much better off will I be if I bring you in instead of working things out with my own people?
▪ How much better are you than your competitors?

In order to approach zero risk, a customer manager must know a comanager's answers beforehand. The customer manager must know how much lower his defect rate will be or how much higher he can expect his productivity or turnover to be. The customer manager must know how much faster his design-to-development cycle or order-to-shipment cycle or time-to-market will turn out to be because these are the improvements he is open to buy. They are therefore the improvements that a comanager must propose, making each proposal customer-specific in ways such as these:

- A comanager's profit proposal to an R&D manager must provide a compelling answer to the question: How much improvement do you normally contribute to the product development cycle time of my kind of products?
- A comanager's profit proposal to a manufacturing manager must provide a compelling answer to the question: How much improvement do you normally contribute to the scrap-to-commercial-output ratio of my kind of products or to the labor content of my kind of materials-handling process?

In each case, a customer's current performance is the comanager's "before" benchmark. The difference between the benchmark and the comanaged "after" outcome represents the value added by the comanager—in other words, his *product* on which his added value is measured and for which he is paid.

Comanagers' outcomes are the result of applying technology, not manufacturing it or selling it. They take a technology such as preventive maintenance and apply it to reduce a customer's downtime. Or they take the technologies of Total Quality Management (TQM) and apply them to reduce a customer's scrap.

Applications data are the source of a comanager's norms, the aggregate of his or her normal contributions of improvement. Because norms are the only personal element that remains in business—everything else has been homogenized, commoditized, and institutionalized—they attest to a comanager's professional expertise as someone a customer manager feels compelled to have on his side. A customer knows what he is getting when a comanager proposes to him like this:

> What if the annual contribution to Plant A gross margin being made by your production process can be brought closer to our norm of $1 million as a result of:
>
> 1. Reducing labor, materials, and manufacturing costs by $350,000 from decreased scrap resulting from off-spec production.
> 2. Reducing maintenance and repair costs by $230,000 from decreased downtime.
> 3. Increasing revenues by $420,000 from improved throughput of marketable goods.
>
> The total $1 million of improved gross profits will be achieved with an investment of $500,000 paid back within nine months, at an internal rate of return of 200 percent.

The only way that a customer manager can know what he is bargaining for is to know the comanager's track record that is expressed by his norms. Similarly, the only way that a comanager can know if he should propose to a customer manager is by comparing his norms against the indicators of a customer's current performance. Where his norms win, there is a proposal opportunity.

Targeting Proposals From KPI Data

Key performance indicators are position-specific for each customer manager and specific to his or her industry. For example, a hospital manager's KPIs are shown as Figure 5-1. No Tier 1 comanager can propose to anyone in hospital management without knowing how to improve such critical success factors as the manager's occupancy rate and by how much he can expect to increase it or how to reduce the average cost per discharged patient and by how much he can expect to reduce it.

Figure 5-1. Hospital manager: key performance indicators.

Capacity Utilization

    Number of beds in service
    Number of total discharges
    Percent occupancy rate
    Number of days average length of stay

Productivity

    Number of personnel per average daily census
    Number of personnel per one hundred discharges
    Percentage of discharges per bed
    Salary and benefit expense as percentage of overhead expenses

Revenues and Expenses

    Gross revenue per discharge
    Operating revenue per discharge
    Expense per discharge
    Percent operating profit margin
    Percent total profit margin
    Percent return on assets
    Cash flow per bed

Comanagers target their proposals by "norm scanning" through two databases. One contains their customers' current financial performance according to each industry's key indicators. This database applies alike to line of business managers and business function managers. The second database contains the business function managers' current operating performance indicators.

The first database may be called an "Investment Productivity Database" because it shows how productively a manager is investing each dollar's worth of assets. The second database may be called an "Operations Contribution Database" because it shows a manager's contribution to revenues or a business function manager's contribution to the cost of earning them.

A comanager's norm-scanning through the two databases is simulated below:

1. Investment productivity database on a manager's financial performance

An asterisk (*) shows KPIs that you can apply to both profit center and cost center managers. A double asterisk (**) applies only to profit center managers.

1.1. *Proposal targets from a manager's key financial performance*

- Is our normal range of total revenues (the sum of all receipts from sales) higher than the customer's current performance?**
- Is our normal range of total operating income (pretax net revenues) higher than the customer's current performance?**
- Is our normal range of cost of goods sold (the sum of sales force salaries and commissions, T&E, and sales support services) lower than the customer's current performance?*

1.2. *Proposal targets from a manager's key operating performance*

- Is our normal ratio of the cost of goods sold to total revenues (gross profits) lower than the customer's current performance?*
- Is our normal ratio of aftertax net income to net sales (net profit) higher than the customer's current performance?**
- Is our normal ratio of the number of employees to total sales revenues (productivity) lower than the customer's current performance?*
- Is our normal ratio of cost of sales or finished goods inventory or order backlog or accounts receivable to total sales (sales efficiency) lower than the customer's current performance?*
- Is our normal ratio of same-day order fulfilment to total sales revenues (sales efficiency) higher than the customer's current performance?*

1.3. *Proposal targets from a manager's working capital performance*

- Is our normal ratio of end-of-year inventory of finished goods to annual net sales (inventory turnover) lower than the customer's current performance?*

- Is our normal ratio of average dollars of receivables outstanding to net sales revenues (accounts receivables turnover) lower than the customer's current performance?*

2. **Operations contribution database on a manager's operating performance**

   2.1. *Proposal targets from an R&D manager's operating performance*
     - Is our normal ratio of R&D costs to sales revenues lower than the customer's current performance?
     - Is our normal ratio of product design costs to sales revenues lower than the customer's current performance?
     - Is our normal ratio of product development costs (from the end of the design cycle through commercial prototyping) to sales revenues lower than the customer's current performance?
     - Is our normal ratio of new product sales revenues to total sales revenues higher than the customer's current performance?

   2.2. *Proposal targets from a manufacturing manager's operating performance*
     - Is our normal ratio of manufacturing cost to sales revenues lower than the customer's current performance?
     - Is our normal ratio of units returned to units shipped lower than the customer's current performance?
     - Is our normal ratio of marketable product to scrap higher than the customer's current performance?
     - Is our normal ratio of warranty costs to sales revenues lower than the customer's current performance?

   2.3. *Proposal targets from an inventory manager's operating performance*
     - Is our normal ratio of inventory costs to sales revenues lower than the customer's current performance?
     - Is our normal ratio of stockouts to orders lower than the customer's current performance?
     - Is our normal ratio of same-day shipments to orders received higher than the customer's current performance?

- Is our normal ratio of just-in-time shipments to total shipments higher than the customer's current performance?

2.4. *Proposal targets from a sales manager's operating performance*
- Is our normal ratio of sales costs to sales revenues lower than the customer's current performance?
- Is our normal ratio of marketing costs to sales revenues lower than the customer's current performance?
- Is our normal ratio of sales closed to sales proposed higher than the customer's current performance?

Becoming Process Smart

A manager's operating performance is a function of two things: costs contributed by the work that flows through each process under his or her control, and costs of the time it takes to complete each work cycle.

Fewer steps in a work flow cost less. Faster cycle times cost less and, by improving the opportunity to be first to market, can contribute to customer revenues. More work done at each workstation costs less. It can also make a revenue contribution. Higher quality work contributes less cost of rework or refund and can justify higher prices. These are the types of benefits that comanagers try to deliver through their profit projects. Work flow data are proposable data. Every profit project affects a work flow, either its integration or its timing. Figures 5-2 and 5-3 show the work flows of two typical customer processes. In Figure 5-2, data are shown the way they currently flow through a distributor customer's order processing system. The flow of a manufacturing customer's product design process is shown in Figure 5-3.

If you are a Tier 1 and you affect either one of these processes, your comanagers are smart about them. They "know the flow." They know the time and money costs that flow through the data processing operation of a distributor, and they know how to save some of those costs by getting to delivery faster. In the product design operation, they know how to get a product

Figure 5-2. Data processing work flow.

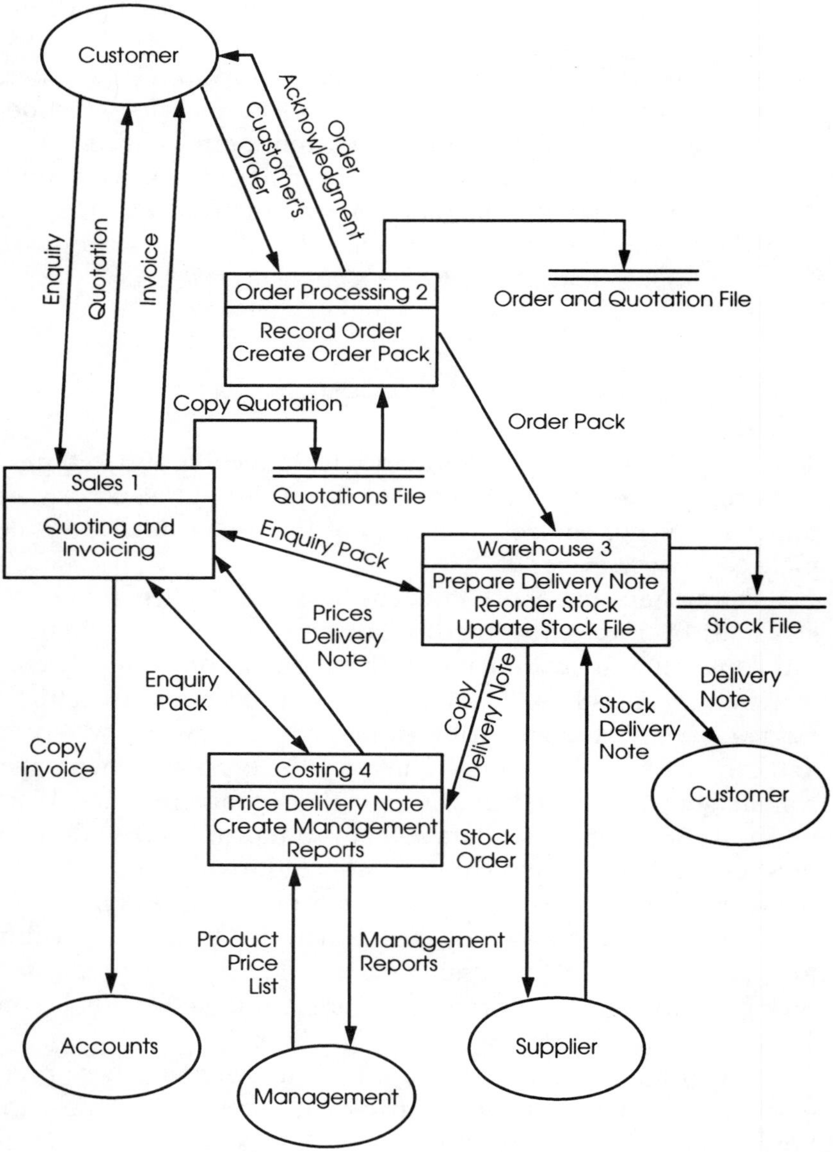

Figure 5-3. Design process work flow.

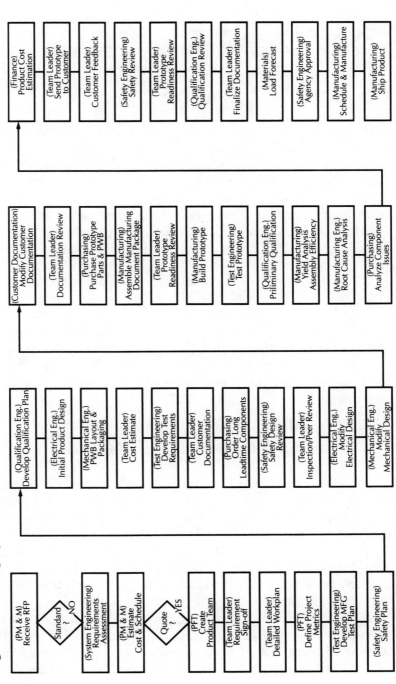

shipped thirty, sixty, or ninety days earlier to bring in revenues faster by accelerating the billing and collections cycle.

Cycling Data Flow

Every profit project's outcome creates a new improved benchmark for customer performance. This raises the bar for the co-manager's next proposal to continue the improvement of his or her customer's competitiveness.

Figure 5-4 shows how a comanager can keep cycling data from benchmark to outcome and from outcome to the next benchmark. Each profit project's end point is the next project's starting point. Each project's midpoint is the planning point for its successor project.

There is no end to the continuity of a comanager's data cycling because his customer-clients' costs can never be low enough and customer revenues can never be high enough no matter how many times they are improved. Costs always rise and revenues are always at risk as new competitors crop up and old standards of performance fade away. Customers improve their management skills, and comanagers must always keep one step ahead.

Siloing Customer Concentration

Large businesses whose economies of scale give them a competitive advantage in the costs of their manufacturing and processing operations are disadvantaged when it comes to doing business in SalesWorld 2000. Ever since horizontal selling began to produce more costs than profits, megacorporations have found themselves with warehouses of square products that no longer fit into the holes of round market segments that look like silos. Nor are they finding a fit with their databases.

Markets have been growing increasingly parochial in their insistence that they be treated as individually distinct entities worthy of being served head-on rather than peripherally. Some of their sense of market-specificity comes from the need to be

Figure 5-4. Recycled data flow.

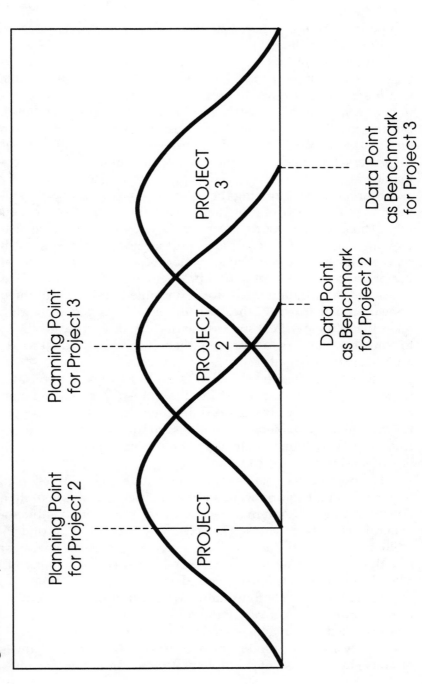

competitively differentiated in their own markets. The rest is economic nationalism.

Progressively finite markets are claiming product and service customization from their suppliers. In response, flexible manufacturing systems are producing variable batches of products with minimum or nearly zero set-up and take-down times. But this is a Tier 2 reaction. Tier 1 businesses serving more than one market require flexible data systems with variable batches of process knowledge for the use of their market-specific co-managers.

Markets are organizing themselves as narrow and deep cylinders. Within each one of them, operating processes of their major business functions are discrete enough to require that their managers abide by unique performance indicators. Each market silo has its own industry norms, its own standards of performance, its own set of best practices, and its own Standard Industry Classification (SIC). To an untrained eye, some of them appear similar to each other. But up close, where comanaging takes place, their critical success factors are sufficiently localized to constitute barriers to entry into them if their individual needs are not acknowledged.

SIC 33 classifies the Primary Metal Industries. If you claim to be generally process-smart in "the industry," you are going backward in time to the era of horizontal marketing. You may not realize it, or suspect that you are fatally disadvantaged because of it, until you run up against a vertical niche specialist in one of its seven 3-digit codes.

Ferrous metals, managers in this market silo will tell you, require different solutions, or solutions differently applied, than nonferrous metals. You may be able to get away with combining general expertise in codes 333 and 334—Primary & Secondary Nonferrous Metals—but you will lose your shirt to the specialist in either code 332 whose silo is Iron & Steel Foundries or code 336 whose silo is Nonferrous Foundries.

Specifications, configurations, or application and installation requirements can vary enough within the same SIC silo to give even niched comanagers a run for their money. In one operation, they may encounter above-average engineering changes or above-average use of multiple materials; yet in another, they will have to know how to deal with short production runs that depend on rapid, multiple customized setups.

Comanagers who consult within a single silo always have the competitive advantage, especially if they have come out of the silo's segment with an operating manager's experience. If so, they speak a silo manager's language. They know his key performance indicators and how to affect them. Above all, they know better than to try to convince a silo manager that his business is not all that different.

6

Distribution Shock: The End of Multivendor Shopping

In one industry after another—from computers, telecommunications, and pharmaceuticals to consumer packaged goods—customers have seized control over the way that goods and services are transacted with their suppliers.

In SalesWorld 2000, account management has been shifted to the demand side. Account control is being transformed into supplier control, which gives customers the power to put a supplier in business as a Tier 1, dictate the terms and conditions that can keep him there or kiss him goodbye when a better comanager—not a better product or service or system—comes along.

Taking customer satisfaction into their own hands, customers have been empowering suppliers to take on some of the functions they used to perform for themselves. One of the functions that customers are outsourcing is purchasing. When you are a Tier 1, you take on your customer-clients' acquisition role by becoming a single-source distributor of their total product and service requirements in your category. For customer-clients, multivendor shopping has ended.

As a Tier 1 comanager, you become a one-stop retailer. If you are a manufacturer, you can continue to supply your house brands along with the products and services of other manufacturers that fill out your lines and complement your systems. Alternatively, you can be a "pure play" supplier of the products and services of multiple manufacturers if you are not a manufacturer yourself.

In either event, you must be source-neutral in your recommendations, prescribing only products and services that are best-in-class for each customer application. Your commitment is to be their integrator into the optimal mix, the supporter and maintainer of their operations, the trainer of the customer people who run them, and the comanager of their outcomes.

Distributing or Being Distributed

The convergence of selling into distribution is a customer-driven strategy. It satisfies three customer needs:

1. The customer can downsize his purchasing functions and their costs, replacing one-on-one multivendor deals with a single-source responsibility for all acquisitions in one or more product or service categories.
2. The customer can gain access to the universe of all available options that can give him his preferred combination of best practices and best cost-effectiveness.
3. The customer can receive applications expertise to help implement his acquired products and services, integrating them initially for maximum productivity and continually upgrading them to maintain a state-of-the-art level of performance. This enables the customer to downsize his or her internal applications and support staffs, replacing insources who are on payroll with a single outsource.

The correlates of these benefits are equally advantageous to a comanager-distributor:

1. The distributor can gain the single-source "last touch" access that he must have in order to establish a long-term partnership.
2. The distributor can gain access to the sum total of all the customer needs in his category that would otherwise by parceled out among dozens to hundreds of individual vendors.
3. The distributor can brand his margin-bearing intellectual

capital in the outcome categories he can improve from
integrating a customer's operating systems, re-engineering his processes, and managing his facilities or product
categories.

These win-win advantages to both sides have parallel advantages in the reductions of sales and support costs for each
distributor's multiple Tier 2 vendors. They are able to focus on
the core competencies that can help them become low-cost,
high-quality, and high-productivity suppliers.

The ascendancy of distributor power over manufacturers
and their sales forces is a major differentiator of SalesWorld
2000, setting it apart. For the first time, whoever controls an industry's channels of distribution—whether for goods, services,
or information—controls the industry's customer relationships.
With this single stroke, the creation of value undergoes a revolu-
tionary shift. No longer is value created at a supplier's point of
production. It has become a product of end customers' points of
application.

Procter & Gamble (P&G) makes Crest toothpaste but Wal-
Mart is the distributor who owns P&G's toothpaste-using customers. Home Depot owns the end users of the manufacturers
who supply its stores in the same way that Charles Schwab owns
the investors in the many makes of financial products he distrib-
utes. Through its Windows 95 software program, Microsoft
owns the Internet users of other suppliers' on-line services.

Whether by human interface or computer, telemarketing,
television shopping, or retail marketing, distributors can offer
end users an array of integrated systems of goods and services
without ever having to take title to them. In this way, they have
become the first force to be able to own markets without owning
the assets required to produce their supplies or even owning the
supplies themselves.

If you decide not to take on the distributor function and
retain manufacturing or a role as service provider as your core
competency, someone else will become the distributor to your
market segment. The distributor, who may be a competitor, will
become your customer. He will be the last business you touch in

his role as agent for your former end-user customers to whom you no longer have direct access.

If you become one of the distributor's preferred suppliers, he will set your price and stipulate your terms and conditions. If he does not prefer you, it will cost you two customers: your original end-user customer and his Tier 1 distributor. The choice is clear: *Distribute or be distributed.*

Getting Proprietary Values From Standard Parts

In order to be a distributor, you must acquire scoping skills to size up customer problems and opportunities, contracting skills to manage profit improvement projects to solve the problems and seize the opportunities, integration skills to mix competitive and supplemental products and services with each other and your own, application skills to integrate the mix into a customer's operations, measurement skills to evaluate the incremental contribution the mix is making to customer profits, and proposal skills to obtain funds to migrate to the next project. In other words, you must become *consultative.*

Distributors may or may not be manufacturers. Either way, they act as outsourced marketers for the Tier 2 manufacturers whose products and services they correlate and integrate. For their client-customers, distributors also perform an outsource function of providing off-the-books external management of purchasing, inventory, information processing, payables invoicing, training, and operations functions.

These functions may be thought of as outsourced noncore capabilities. By outsourcing them, customers are free to focus on the outbound aspects of their businesses represented by the profit-center operations that bring money in rather than the inbound cost centers that expend it.

Most of the products and services you contract for will be tried-and-true performers whose contributions have been made predictable by a long-term track record. You will be an assembler of commodity parts because, like your client-customers, you can accept only zero risk. Your margins come from your brandable ability to add value to commodity systems in one or more of three ways:

1. You get greater proprietary values out of them than anyone else, which means that you set the standard for value.
2. You get faster standard values out of them than anyone else.
3. You get standard values out of them at lower cost than anyone else.

The standard of a distributor's performance is met when only the contributions he makes to customer outcomes are made visible; when his product and service mix and his mixing skills remain behind the scenes because they are never featured, never priced, and therefore never sold. If they were featured, they would have to be priced. If they were priced, they would have to be discounted.

Distributors add their value as appliers, not suppliers. Their motto is "More Better Faster Outcomes" for their customers. By using their "applications smarts"—the impact from putting their intellectual capital to work on their "process smarts" about customer operations—they get to outcome through the five-step sequence shown in Figure 6-1.

1. Their norms enable them to target leads for profit projects.
2. Their diagnostic skills create proposal opportunities out of leads.
3. Their prescriptive skills predict improved outcomes from implementing their proposals.
4. Their application smarts help them to realize their proposed outcomes.
5. Their ability to use each improved outcome as the benchmark for the next profit project enables them to deliver continuously improved outcomes.

Managing Tier 2 Supply Chains

Comanagers must ensure their Tier 2 sources of supply. This means that they must have market knowledge of current best-

Figure 6-1. Critical path to "get to outcome."

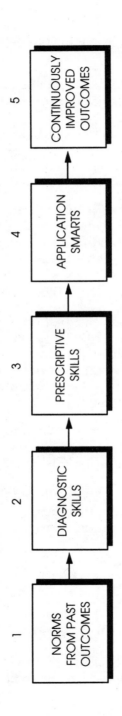

in-class technologies and their most likely emergent successors. They also must have partnering ability to make third-party and multiparty strategic alliances with diverse skillholders and service providers, manage them in virtual networks, and maximize their contributions.

In order to own best practices in marshalling the most cost-effective mixes of enabling technologies, you must be a good supply-chain manager. Your Tier 2 portfolio must be composed of highly productive, tightly cost-controlled, and zero-defect quality suppliers. They must be able to manage your inventory requirements for both just-in-time delivery and just-in-case warehousing, centralize their billing procedures, maintain quick response to your unscheduled needs, and service the products and subsystems they supply. In turn, they must also be good supply-chain managers of their own sources.

Your supply-chain management must be a backroom operation. Your customer-clients should never be aware of it, nor should they be aware of the suppliers who compose it. Only their technical people should know the brand names you integrate and only as a reality check to confirm your sourcing skills. Tier 2 brand names are otherwise irrelevant. With equality of quality and each brand good enough to make its required contribution to the mix, its component parts all may be thought of as coming from an old reliable East Asian company named "Hu Cares."

Distributors are in an ideal position to take advantage of product anonymity. On the supplier end of their business, they use it to buy at low cost. On the buyer end, they bundle the cost in a capabilities package that is represented by the fee for outcome. No single-source seller can match them. One channel flows upstream and provides a distributor with exclusive access to one or more of a customer's critical operating functions and lines of business. He is the sole supplier to touch the customer. Flowing downstream, the second channel opens up global access to all the goods and services that a distributor may want to call on to provide the most cost-effective mix for each customer-client.

In information technology, EDS is a model Tier 1 distributor for computer and telecommunications hardware, software, and services. In consumer packaged goods, Wal-Mart is a model distributor. In the case of EDS, added value comes from prescribing the optimal product mix for each customer, integrating it into a cost-effective system, maintaining and upgrading it for continuous improvement, and managing its performance. Wal-Mart's added value is twofold: it comes from touching its suppliers' customers in the most convenient, cost-effective manner. In addition, it customer-orients its manufacturers by informing their research and development, package design, in-store promotion, and just-in-time inventory management with customer needs, wants, and desires.

Touching the Customer Last

Manufacturers who aspire to Tier 1 status must either become distributors or acquire a distributor in order to establish a direct link to their market shares. Growth in SalesWorld 2000 is driven more by distribution than by manufacturing or marketing capabilities. It is not owning an aggregate of assets that makes a SalesWorld 2000 business profitable. It is owning last-touch access to customers, who turn out to be the only assets worth owning because they are the ultimate source of funds.

Two examples show how distribution is overtaking sales in two different industries:

1. In discount brokerage, Charles Schwab has become a distributor for hundreds of mutual funds. Seeing that his industry's power has been shifting from the manufacturers of funds to the channelers of their access—from makers of products to makers of markets—he has created One Source to provide one-stop shopping for any fund for which he can make a market.

Thinking of One Source as a financial Wal-Mart, Schwab says that "We're not out to manufacture funds but to distribute them."

For One Source's customers, One Source is their sole supplier. They touch no other source, which endows Schwab with ownership of their relationships. Fund manufacturers receive several trade-offs. In Tier 2 fashion, they cut their sales costs, free themselves from the penalties of their marketing inefficiencies, and profit from the expanded selling and cross-selling opportunities that One Source opens up for them.

2. In pharmaceuticals, Merck, the world's largest manufacturer, acquired Medco Containment Services, the largest U.S. mail order drug distributor known as a drug-benefit manager. The "containment" in Medco's name stands for cost containment. Based on its ability to help control drug costs, Medco had been positioning itself between Merck and its major markets among health maintenance organizations (HMOs), labor unions, Fortune 500 corporations, and other mass-purchasing medical plan sponsors. As a result, Medco held Merck at its mercy by controlling the Merck products that made it onto a customer's preferred-drug lists. Medco also required Merck to discount its prices if it wanted to maintain volume.

Medco currently acts as a One Source for all pharmaceutical products, not just products manufactured by Merck. Medco buys wherever its managers get the best prices, locking out its competitors by guaranteeing dollar-specific savings. In order to know where to set its guarantees of the costs that can be contained, Medco maintains a computerized patient research database to track the efficacy of the drugs it sells. In return for its guarantee, Medco earns the right to have a say in how customers manage their diagnosis, treatment, and home-health aftercare of each drug's patients. More drugs get sold this way. As a result, Medco emerges as the surviving Tier 1 consultant whereas its acquirer, Merck, becomes one of Medco's Tier 2 suppliers.

By the year 2000, Merck plans to channel 80 percent or more of its volume through Medco. When that happens, Merck's 5,500 sales representatives at the time of Medco's acquisition will no longer be needed to call on individual practice physicians, doctors' groups, and hospitals, several of them often calling on the same customer. Another sales force will disappear.

7

Keiretsu Shock: The End of Supplier Competition

Venerable institutions such as vendor selling, like old soldiers, die by fading away. As the end nears, they go through a final act of passage by debating what is by then no longer debatable but would have been too hot for them to handle at an earlier time when something might have been done.

For most Tier 2 sales forces, it has been a progressive process, with an air of inevitability about its conclusion in eliminating the institution along with the debate.

In the 1960s and 1970s, sales forces whose products and services were well on the way to becoming commodities fiddled while Rome burned by debating whether or not they were at prospective risk of commoditization. The Continental and American Can companies maintained a mutual state of denial about the commodity nature of their products by pointing to their continuous parallel innovations. One's pop-top closure matched the other's. One's EconoWeld invisible seam matched the other's Miraseam. Customers ran their fingers over the seams they could not see and marvelled at the miracles of can-making technology while they discounted the can companies' margins until they were even less visible than the seams.

In the services business, Big Eight accounting firms wasted the entire decade of the 1970s in speculation that their bread and butter, the annual recurring audit that was the basis of their entire assurance business, might be on the way to becoming a commodity. Long before, however, all eight firms had been buying business with their audits instead of selling it. The "Lybrand Method" of Coopers & Lybrand was buttressed top to bottom with checks and balances that suggested superior competitive value but consistent acknowledgment of that value was hard to find when a client signed the check.

So all-pervasive was commoditization by the end of the 1970s that sales forces recognized the parity of their products, processes, and proposals by looking everywhere for what they called a "tiebreaker"—anything that could give them the slightest edge in competitions that began even-up and often ended the same way.

Floor-to-ceiling checklists of distinctions without a difference offered no extra points to customers who knew, even if their suppliers did not, that feature for feature, benefit for benefit, and discount for discount, sameness was endemic and no amount of "selling harder" could pretend otherwise.

In the years that followed, sales forces of the most inward-looking companies—those whose businesses originated with engineers, where the laboratory was their shrine, and whose internal functions never talked to one another and were always at war, leaving their customers on the sidelines—began a second wave of introspection. "Write down ten ways in which we are customer-driven," Hewlett-Packard asked its 1980s sales force, most of whom held electronic engineering degrees and were being rewarded for selling their technology on its price and performance with no thought of the customer value it might be able to convey.

Throughout the 1980s, it was customers such as Wal-Mart and not their suppliers like Procter & Gamble, it was the Medcos and not their suppliers like Merck, who were taking leadership in customer-driving. When vendors came around to it at all, they came kicking and screaming.

Becoming Organizationally Built-In

With the major issues disposed of—yes, they were commoditized and no, they were not customer-driven—vendor sales forces entered the 1990s with only a single hair left to split. Were they makers of transaction sales or relationship sales? At this point, many Tier 2 businesses were becoming terminal. Disguising their sales representatives as "relationship managers," they larded over their transaction sales with the added costs and inefficiencies of diffusing what little customer knowledge they had and diluting account responsibility among relationship managers, account managers, customer satisfaction managers, service managers, and support managers.

Few of these pseudopartnerships have ever paid off because they lack the currency of true business partnership, which is an exchange of value between the partners. As late as the mid-1990s, it was commonplace for Fortune 500 sales forces to be totally ignorant of their added value. At Xerox, for example, color copying machines were being priced at a 25 percent premium. When Xerox sales representatives were challenged to justify the premium, they responded the way they had been taught: They said that they *felt* color would improve a customer's response rate from promotional mailings, perhaps by as much as 25 percent. But no one taught them how to quantify their feelings in terms of the most likely dollar value of the improved response rate and, as an index of its quality, how many of the added responses would most likely be convertible into customers. As a result, the only value they were able to quantify was the added cost of color. Because the scenario of proposing the added cost of color and being rejected soon became predictable, the Xerox representatives were also taught how to petition their managers for a 10 percent price break. The managers were simultaneously taught how to resist it.

At the same time, account management processes throughout the Fortune 500 typically began each sales cycle with a "step one" that counselled "understanding the customer's business issues and opportunities." But few salespeople knew their customers' middle-management issueholders, either who they were or where to find them, let alone being aware of their issues. Tying a sale to a business issue became a commercial version of pin-the-tail-on-the-donkey. Sales proposals, whether they were authentic donkey tails or not, were haphazardly stuck onto a business issue's backside. When the business issue coughed, the sales proposals fell off.

Vendor sales forces, it turned out, were working at the wrong end. As SalesWorld 2000 approached, Tier 1 comanagers were taking business issues by the bit and leading customer-clients head-first toward their objectives.

Tier 1 comanagers were not waking up an hour earlier one morning because a request for proposal had come in the night before and they had to take a crash course in the buzzwords of a customer's business. They already knew the business. As permanent residents in the flow of customer business issues and objectives, comanagers were sharing the same total immersion as their customers and doing it with them in real time. There is no way they could avoid it because they were being organizationally built into the operations they comanaged; they were contributing improved performance rather than maintaining improved relations.

Joining Together Complementary Capabilities

The comanager's operational interdependence with his customers, while he himself remains independent, is reminiscent of the Japanese *keiretsu*. The production model of keiretsu, as distinguished from the financial model of interlocking trading conglomerates centered on a bank, is an informal linkage. It joins the complementary capabilities of multiple supplier organizations and their customers and manages them for mutual benefits over long periods of time.

In the SalesWorld 2000 concept of keiretsu, it is an interpersonal integration, webbing together Tier 1 comanagers with customer managers in the same way that systems integration creates networks of operating functions. Keiretsu is a coordinating strategy that achieves many of the benefits of an internal vertical integration, yet preserves the freedom to go outside for independent counsel and sourcing. In other words, it provides a combination of arms-around with arm's-length.

Keiretsuing enables a comanager to learn a customer's business from the customer. He or she does not need public sources for understanding. As an insider, the comanager is privy. Customers trade off their proprietary knowledge to him in return for his putting it to work for the continuous improvement of their performance in the operations he affects. On a one-to-one basis, they can add value to their competitiveness. Their added values are in the form of their comanagers' consultation, application, implementation, and information.

The comanager's predictability as a reliable profit improver is a customer's principal justification for accepting him as a virtual vertical integration. Unlike a totally controlled resource, however, a comanager's independence puts him perpetually under the gun to innovate, to enhance cost-effectiveness as a member of customer management without portfolio, and to compete, if not against other suppliers, against his own most recent best contributions. The comanager's incentive is ongoing because his tenure is at the customer's satisfaction.

In the intermediate position between being owned by the customer and being an alternate supplier on the open market, a comanager combines the best aspects of third-party autonomy in his or her ability to prescribe uncommon solutions, open access to the entire competitive marketplace for sourcing, and the outsider's continuous incentive while avoiding the worst aspects of customer corporate bureaucracy.

A comanager's position is neither first-party like his customer-client nor third-party like an alternate vendor. Somewhere in between, the comanager is a first-party "line extension." No vendor can get as close. No vendor's ticket is punched with the same breadth and depth of knowledge of the customer.

A comanager's added value comes from stable, sustainable growth partnerships. Keiretsu partners achieve stability through open relationships, which are miniature correlates of an open market. Within a keiretsu, information flows freely. But privileged access to knowledge has its price. Continuity is earned by compliance with promise. Compliance is assured by the ongoing measurement of a comanager's performance as value adder and contributor to the key indicators of his or her customer-client's performance. Quality standards are enforced. There is no privacy. In an open relationship, there is no place to hide.

Constructively Ending Supplier Competition

Keiretsu-type comanagement constructively ends competition among Tier 1 suppliers for a customer-client's business. Competition all along the value chain is even further diminished by the keiretsu relationships established between Tier 1 and its Tier 2 suppliers. Tier 1-Tier 2 keiretsus are long-term strategic alliances that create the virtual organizations shown in Figure 1-6.

Paradoxically, the competitiveness of customers at the top of the value chain is accelerated by the end of supplier competition. The back-and-forth sharing of information between comanagers and their providers, and between comanagers and their customers, increases the rate of successful projects as well as their rates of return.

A keiretsued comanager has every reason to be reliable. He shares proportionately in the keiretsu's gain. He has every encouragement to participate in the initiatives that his customers propose as well as proposing new ventures and incremental improvements in established operations. His incentives are never constrained by whether or not he has a product he can sell or if he can be paid enough for his product to recapture the cost of his services. Nor does he have to put a price on his services and thereby commoditize them. Few if any vendors can make these claims.

An axiom of SalesWorld 2000 says that keiretsu partnerships tend to remain in partnership. A corollary axiom says that customers not yet in keiretsu partnerships tend not to remain unpartnered for long. When they partner, they tend to remain partnered.

It is a fact of SalesWorld 2000 life that a customer's competitiveness cannot be maximized by competition among his Tier 1 suppliers. Under such competition, project fees would become negotiable. Creative inspiration, perhaps leading to sporadically innovative solutions, might also be provoked. But these apparent advantages would be nullified by the absence of deep-dish customer knowledge—which is the basis for creativity over the long term—that can be acquired only in the privileged partnerships of keiretsus. Without it, a competitive supplier's applications expertise would be sufficiently devalued to impair the magnitude and certainty of each proposed solution's outcome.

If keiretsu partners do their jobs, they are at risk to no one but themselves. Neither of them is likely to be replaced unless the customer partner leaves or is promoted or the comanager partner becomes vulnerable to a competitive comanager's superior norms for improved customer performance. Mutual growth is the source of keiretsu staying power for as long as no better grower emerges on either side.

The insider second-party nature of comanagement tends to lock up customers and lock out competitors. The opportunity for customer conversion by tried-and-true propositions based on lower prices or higher technologies is forestalled. Only proof of significantly improved outcomes can make a difference. In its absence, partnered pairs of comanagers and their customer managers tend to perpetuate themselves.

Searching for the Smallest Success Factors

As the keiretsu model of mating-not-quite-for-life increases and tilts the traditional playing field toward transient monopolies, new opportunities to become a player are, as if in compensation, exploding exponentially.

No comanager, or any Tier 1 company of comanagers, can be the leading standardbearer of continuous improvement in many things, let alone everything. Any attempt to do so, whether by pushing the envelopes of applications expertise until they break or merging with or acquiring endless extensions of a core expertise, would create the same kind of unmanageable monster that caused the old Enterprise business model shown in Figure 1-3 to atomize into Tier 1 and Tier 2.

The opportunistic comanagers of SalesWorld 2000 are master segmenters of their customers' operations. They continually niche and microniche profit centers and cost centers in search of the smallest practicable success factors over which to take ownership. At the same time, they continually network their niches in search of the most comprehensive systems their niched expertise can contribute to. In this way, they combine a keyhole focus on realizable customer objectives with a grandview understanding of just how they affect the transcendent business issues that the objectives serve. To the extent that they are motivated to expand laterally into one or more adjacent niches to contribute to more segments of their networks, keiretsu comanagers become balancers of risk and reward—managers who have come a long way from their original sales heritage of merely balancing price and performance.

Among comanagers, he or she who niches finitely niches best. Knowing "everything about something"—that is, being a generalist in a specialty—is the sole successful strategy for consistently putting up world-class results. Because SalesWorld 2000 is customer operation-driven, the competitiveness of each critical-to-success function or process is every customer's predominant need. This is why customers reach out to Tier 1 and not Tier 2. If the outcome from operations is to be enhanced, the comanager's applications expertise becomes the supercritical resource.

In a world where the competitiveness of customers supersedes the competitiveness of their suppliers, the one-operation comanager—or, at most, the one integrated system of operations comanager—is king.

8

Gainsharing Shock: The End of Price

Comanagers must represent zero cost to their customer-clients. This means that they cannot ask to be paid a price for the products, services, or systems they apply. Nor can they ask to be paid a fee in the form of an hourly rate for their consultation, information, education, implementation, or evaluation of results from their profit projects. Instead, comanagers ask to be paid a share of the gains they contribute to the key performance indicators of their customer-clients.

The acronym for a comanager's gainsharing is VIVO: *Value In* to the comanager depends on *Value Out* to the customer. Since value is outcome-dependent, gainsharing makes a comanager's compensation specific to the results of his or her applications rather than product-specific, service-specific, or system-specific. The improvement in competitiveness of customer functions, operations, and processes becomes the source of comanagement compensation.

Making customers better competitors—better earners of revenues at better revenue-to-investment ratios—has superseded making products or services better as a comanager's number one objective. As a result, price as a medium of exchange has ended at Tier 1, replaced by value. Price continues to exist only at Tier 2 and even there it is imposed downward from Tier 1.

In a world lacking differentiation, the only rational basis for price is the value you add and not the cost you incur. Value is the sole deliverable that can be differentiated because it is the result of goods and services being *applied*, not simply *supplied*. Application, unlike products, can be individualized by the applier so that its result differs from the results of all other appliers, even those who implement similar goods and services.

Whereas products, services, and systems are available everywhere at comparable quality, and everywhere the same terms and conditions, only value enjoys uniqueness and, at consistently high levels of delivery, is always in short supply.

No customer can ever have enough value added to his operations. That is why it is dear to him. The way that comanagers make money is to price what is dear and not what is free.

- Quality is free. It is free because everyone offers it at equally acceptable levels. Beyond the point of customer satisfaction known as "good enough," surplus quality adds no reclaimable value. Quality at the level of equality is a commodity. If you try to base your price on quality, it will be discounted to the lowest common denominator of all the quality suppliers in your market. You will end up giving your quality away as if it were free—the same result as not pricing your quality in the first place.

- Technology is free. It is free because everyone in the same industry offers the same technology. Any unique technology becomes commonplace before long. It has the same foreshortened life as its products. Its low price of entry is no barrier, either to making it or to buying it outside. Technology is a commodity. If you try to base your price on technology, it will be discounted to the lowest common denominator of all the technology supplied to your market. You will end up giving your technology away as if it were free—the same result as not pricing your technology in the first place.

In the same way, product-related services are free; customer training is free; just-in-time delivery is free; and additional once-upon-a-time priceable benefits become free every day. Since they cannot be sold at margins based on their added value, no sales force can afford to sell them.

As a Tier 1, gainsharing meets your customer-clients' needs because the only way to realize zero cost is through zero price. By substituting pay for performance for pay for products or services—in other words, pay for value instead of pay for cost—gainsharing puts an end to cost. What used to be a customer's acquisition cost becomes an investment on which there is a shared return. As soon as the customer's investment is paid back, it takes on the nature of a short-term loan whose "interest rate" compensates both the customer and his comanager for their contributions.

Putting Your Own Skin in the Game

Baxter Healthcare Corporation is becoming a SalesWorld 2000 Tier 1 by creating a menu of gainsharing choices for doing business with its hospital customers. In its partnership with Allegheny Health Foundation, Baxter gains a percentage of the savings it contributes to the management of each of the foundation's member hospital's inventory of surgical supplies. For another customer, Duke University Medical Center, Baxter is basing its gainsharing agreement on managing the total costs of the center's surgical supplies. As supply comanager, Baxter guarantees an annual ceiling on Duke's expenditures in return for a comanager's fee. If Duke's costs come out higher than the ceiling, Baxter pays the overrun. If Duke's costs are less than Baxter's guarantee, Baxter is compensated by a share of the savings. In either case, Baxter avoids discounting its margins by removing price from its products. It also avoids competition by comanaging its customers' supply operations. At the same time, Duke benefits by getting out of paying for overpurchasing, cost-ineffective inventory management, and wasteful consumption, as well as avoiding the duplicate costs of dealing with multiple vendors.

Under all arrangements of gainsharing, *paying is the result of payoff.* The comanager gets paid the same way the customer does: on performance.

Pay for performance has made buying and selling products or services obsolete above the Tier 2 level because it makes them irrelevant as the basis for price. At Tier 1, your costs and the capabilities they support remain your own business; they, too, are irrelevant for pricing.

Tier 1's customer-clients pay for a comanager's contribution, not for his costs. Repaying his costs is the comanager's
problem rather than something to be passed along to his customers. Gainsharing puts the comanager's skin in the game.
Risk is shared along with gain. This places the burden on comanagers to prescribe only the most cost-effective solutions instead of the costliest ones. It also ensures that comanagers will
not automatically favor their own products and services if others
can contribute to a greater or quicker or more certain outcome.

Calculating the Gain for Sharing

Gainsharing is based on the incremental contributions you make
as a Tier 1 to your customer-clients' managers on a per-project
basis. Each project should be looked at as a gainmaker. You can
calculate its most likely gain by asking:

- How much positive value can we help a customer-client
  acquire by adding to his revenues?
- How much negative value can we help a customer-client
  eliminate by subtracting from his costs?

The shareable value added to a customer-client is called Direct Project Value (DPV). It attempts to account for a comanager's project-specific contributions more meaningfully than trying
to isolate it from total droppings to a customer's corporate bottom line. Project contributions may be dispersed or dispensed
long before they reach bottom. Besides, top-line contributions to
a line of business manager who is running an emergent new
business or a turnaround for quick buildup of market share may
be even more important than bottom-line residue.

Instead of attempting to identify your added value in the
mishmash of your customer-clients' profit-and-loss statements
or, even more vacuously, in their per-share stock values, your
best bet is to calculate your contributions according to how
much each profit project adds to a customer manager's key performance indicators—in other words, *how much you contribute to
how much your customer-client contributes.*

When it comes to calculating your share of a customer-client's gains, you and your gainpartners must make peace with two facts of comanaged life:

1. Try as you will, you will rarely if ever be able to isolate with precision your comanaged contributions apart from your partner's managed contributions. Rule one says to get used to the fact you will always be working from joint contributions.

2. You will rarely if ever be able to isolate with precision a profit project's contribution from the influence of fortuitous external variables that may inflate your contributions or make it seem that your contributions would have occurred spontaneously without any intervention on your part. Rule two says get used to the fact that you will always be working from assumed contributions.

Benign imprecision is a better basis for agreement than paralytic dissention. All the incremental gains from each profit project should go into a common pot for gainsharing. By the laws of chance, this will result in a fair but inequitable dispensation. A comanager will be overcompensated 50 percent of the time and underpaid the other 50 percent.

As an example, a potential share of the gain from comanaging a profit project can be 20 percent of its gross profit improvement, based on the midpoint of a range from a low end of 10 to 15 percent for very large projects or projects where gross margin is small to a high end of 25 to 35 percent for projects of relatively small return or that pose an extra degree of difficulty.

In this example, a customer manager is presented with a proposition that would read like this if it were to be put into words: "Is it worth investing $2 in my comanagement capabilities to get your hands on $8 out of every $10 added that we can make together?"

In order to "get to yes," the customer manager will have to go through the following thought process:

- Is trading off $2 for every $8 compatible with my normal cost of capital?
- Is $2 for every $8 a good deal, or can I get $8 at the same

risk by paying only $1 to someone else or get back $9 for every $1?
- Is $8 out of every $10 enough cash flow for my needs?

In an alternative scenario, a comanager can approach gain-sharing like this:

- Think of me as if I were your cost of sales. What if you, Ms. line of business manager, share with me a percent equal to your cost per sale for each incremental dollar of revenue that I help generate over and above my proposal?
- Think of me as if I were your cost of capital. What if you, Mr. business function manager, share with me a percent equal to your cost of capital for each incremental dollar of cost I help reduce over and above my proposal?

Guaranteeing the Floor for Gainsharing

Essential to fulfilling a customer's objective of zero cost is the concept of the *harmless comanager*. Before a comanager can do good, he or she must guarantee to do no harm. The customer must always be made whole.

The comanager's strategy for assured wholeness is to guarantee a minimum outcome. The comanager's profit projects must pay off according to plan or the comanager makes up the difference. Either way, the customer achieves his planned outcome. He realizes zero cost. In addition, the customer does so at zero risk. The only risk that remains is the potential opportunity cost from losing out on what might have been even greater returns from alternate opportunities.

For a comanager, risk also should be zero. This can be accomplished by staying always within his norms, the range of improved contributions the comanager normally makes from applying similar types of solutions to similar lines of business or business functions in the customer's industry.

As long as each application meets two requirements, staying within norms should enable a comanager to guarantee his contributions to customer outcomes free of risk to himself:

1. An application must be substantially similar to applications on which his norms are based.
2. An application must not be substantially dissimilar to these applications in any significant way.

If you do not know your norms, you will not be able to guarantee your added value. If you are not able to guarantee your added value, you will not know where to set the floor for gainsharing.

By guaranteeing a customer's *payback*, you promise him zero cost at zero risk. The customer is sure he cannot lose. By guaranteeing a customer's *payout*, you promise him a positive cash flow. The customer is sure to make a preferred investment. In return for your guarantees, you remove the ceiling on your own return. This is your incentive for continuous improvement.

Raising the roof on reward is also your warranty of partnership, rewarding you for your contributions on the same basis as your customer managers. Not only are you paid by the same yardstick; you are paid from the same pool of funds.

Mediating Growth With Shares of Gain

Gainsharing is the acid test of a Tier 1. Claiming to improve customer profits is one thing; doing it is another; being confident enough that you can do it to base your income on it is something else again because it puts a Tier 1's money where its mouth is.

Tier 1s that cannot guarantee minimum outcomes will lose opportunities to those who do. Tier 1s that cannot guarantee the highest minimum outcomes because they do not have the highest rated norms will lose opportunities to those who do. Tier 1s that cannot gainshare because they are unable to guarantee will lose revenues to those who do since gainsharing always should net out a greater reward than pricing. Tier 1s that cannot pay off on meeting their guarantees will disappear from business. All these types of Tier 1 will wither and die, either being acquired by other Tier 1s or falling out of Tier 1 into Tier 2.

Because there is no cap on shared earnings, gainsharing is the only accelerator of growth that is available to a Tier 1. All other ways of making money provide slow or no growth since they position a Tier 1 as an added cost instead of a creator of new wealth. Tier 1s are under constant pressure to grow because they must be able to attract the best intellectual capital for whom pay-for-performance is the only incentive they respond to.

Tier 1's role as a mediator of growth is made clear by gain-sharing. Tier 1s must grow their networks, each of which includes a customer-client and a virtual organization of Tier 2 suppliers. Gainsharing symbolizes Tier 1's responsibility to provide a growth culture for its capital holders, the men and women assets who hold its applications expertise in their hands.

No Tier 1 ever will be better than its people. None of a Tier 1's people ever will be better than the growth culture that must be the driver of their never-ending march toward transient norm supremacy.

Customer gain always must be a Tier 1's reason for existence. Sharing in the gain provides the wherewithal to improve the gain its comanagers can deliver.

9

Dealmaking Shock: The End of Sales Training

The Tier 1 help-providers and care-givers of SalesWorld 2000 who comanage improved outcomes from customer operations are a new breed, more like the customer managers they partner with than the traditional vendor sales representatives they have evolved from. Different as they are from vendors, comanagers are similar to each other in two respects:

1. They have the ability to propose and close investment proposals for profit projects in the form of business cases.
2. They can train their customer-clients to implement profit projects under their comanagement.

These twin standards of comanager performance are unrelated to and largely irrespective of products, services, or systems; their technologies; or any other factor in the comanager's own business. This requires comanagers to be trained in altogether new ways, ending the comic opera that has been passed off as sales training for the past half-century or more.

Even before the thrust of comanagement, sales training by whatever name—professional selling, strategic selling, relationship selling, counselor selling, conceptual selling, or partnership selling—has been, in terms of outcome, philanthropic selling in which margins have been regularly donated for volume.

If you sold "strategically," your strategy became giving

away your margins to a technical buyer. If you sold "conceptually," your strategy would turn out to make your margins purely conceptual. If you sold "relationships," you would find that your dominant relationship was an increasingly inverse ratio between your cost of sales and your margins.

All these approaches have a common denominator. They train sales representatives to be losers, creating loss in their own companies, where they add cost that is uncompensated by a receivable, and in their customer operations, where they lose the opportunity to add value. Instead of teaching men and women who sell how to arm their customers with powerful new streams of cash flow, they advocate trying to disarm customers from thinking, correctly, "Here comes the pitch."

When customers hang tough as soon as they see that they are not going to be enriched, salespeople are taught that it is acceptable for them to walk away. As a practitioner of conceptual selling has said, "I know you can't get to win-win every time. So when we both walked away feeling okay, we both won." But the fact of the matter is that they both lost out on the chance to add value whose worth, or even existence, neither of them will ever know. And the conceptual seller has left behind a sales cost that he or she will never be able to make up.

Training men and women to sell without margin is on borrowed time. Its days are numbered by the declining cost-effectiveness of vendor selling. As a result, vending is being downloaded out of corporate sales forces onto lower overhead third-party resellers and telemarketers just one step ahead of its cost and one step behind its effectiveness. Vendor sales forces will come to an end and vendor training along with it at the moment in time when no human hand or human voice will any longer be an affordable added cost to a product or service.

Vendor selling and the training to prepare for it are going out with a whimper instead of a bang. The whimper is a sales representative's plaintive cry, "Well, what do *you* think a fair price should be?" Once the buyer is given control of price, he becomes the seller. As soon as that happens, the sales representative has negotiated himself out of the selling scenario.

Along with the sellers for whom it has been as much of a treat as a treatment—a "flavor of the month" ranging from "hunting foxes" in January to filling out "blue sheets" in June and wondering what to do next because you have "been there and done that" and you are still giving margin away—vendor sales training is on its way to becoming history. Instead of product-smart vendors being trained to sell features and benefits, an entirely different class of people are undergoing development into clones of the business managers they must partner with to move their companies' goods and services without selling them.

Well before the year 2000, the box sellers of IBM and Xerox will have sold their last computer and copier, the barrel sellers of Exxon will have sold their last barrel of oil, the radio sellers of Motorola will have sold their last two-way radio, the blood-collection sellers of Becton-Dickinson will have sold their last hypodermic needle, and the loan officers of Citibank will have sold their last dollar bill.

Teaching Comanagers to Teach

If you are a Tier 1, your comanagers are the only types of representative in SalesWorld 2000 who touch end-user customers. They touch them at the operating manager level where they are complementary, not adversarial. In mindset and skillset, there should be no way to differentiate one from the other.

Comanagement education must therefore be reciprocal to customer management education. Comanager performance indicators must be the reciprocals of their customer managers' performance indicators. Standards of performance between them must compare one-for-one.

Both by disposition and training, through necessity as well as choice, a comanager must be a teacher. First of all, he or she must teach customer managers how to be more competitive by multiplying their options for profit contribution. In addition, comanagers must teach each manager's people how to manage, measure, and migrate continuously improved performance. They must also teach Tier 2 supplier networks how to maximize their productivity as sources of low-cost, high-quality products and services.

Whether your comanagers are recruited from the customer

industries you do business with or from the re-engineering of your own sales force, you must help them develop the three proficiencies that Mack Hanan teaches in his course on "Consultative Comanagement™":

1. *Project management,* so they can administer a continous stream of comanaged profit projects for profit-center and cost-center managers
2. *Profit-center management,* so they can help line of business managers improve the profits of their product or service lines
3. *Asset management,* so they can help business function managers run their operations more cost-effectively so they can maximize the contributions they make to profit-center managers

This is what "sales training" looks like in SalesWorld 2000. It is a far cry from the old vendor curriculum of overcoming objections, perfecting the ability to say "yes, but," petitioning for the "right to propose," conducting high-school-level "research" on customer buying patterns and politics, and trying to sell reports that allege to scope out customer needs but are really smokescreens to recommend purchase of the supplier's products and services. In SalesWorld 2000, comanagers are not just trained. They are trained to train.

With each profit project, a comanager's moment of maximum risk occurs when he or she hands off the project's command, control, and communications to the customer-client's people. If his transfer of management technology is not seamless, the project's outcome may be imperiled along with the comanager's basis for gainsharing that depends on it. In addition, the comanager's norms will be endangered.

Enabling customer-clients to realize every last dollar of each profit project's benefits must be the key subject for comanager training. A comanager's fate rests in hands he does not own, that do not report to him, that the comanager cannot control with rewards and penalties, and in whose recruitment, training, and motivation he pays little if any role. Yet these are the people every comanager must count on to make his customer-clients more competitively advantaged. How well the comanager is able to train them to implement his skills in the management of his profit projects is a critical factor in his success.

A comanager's training regime for customer-clients' profit project teams should include five components:

1. Standards of performance for each player that are based on key performance indicators
2. A shared reward schedule based on pay for individual and team performance
3. A self-measurement program to evaluate progress at periodic milestone events
4. A database of project strategies and outcomes to be used as the basis for norm creation
5. Continuous comanager consultation to ensure continuous performance improvement

The net result of a comanager's training regime is to teach his customer-clients two subjects: how to work with him and how to go on working in his image without him.

Emerging Into Professionalism

Selling has always been an art form. Its best practitioners have been artists, artfully suspending disbelief while, as many of them have said, "putting a hand into a customer's pocket to remove his wallet." Customers were never supposed to know what had happened, so smooth was the performance. Even when they found out too late to do anything about it, they could still admire the performance.

People who sell have flattered themselves and each other by calling the kind of vendor selling they perform a profession. But selling has never put forth entry requirements, qualifications, or accreditations. No adherence to any institutional standards or practices, with sanctions for violating them, has ever been legislated in the manner of a true profession. "Best practices" have been whatever works best rather than a set of statutes, caveats, and by-laws.

With comanagement comes the possibility of training in ac-credited professional practice. At the least, comanagers must know what to do with their hands. While the left hand may still be in a customer's pocket, the right hand must be in the other pocket putting more money back in than the left hand takes out.

Enforceable standards of practice are no more elusive than standards of performance; indeed, one is the mirror image of the other. A comanager's key performance indicators are suscep-tible to the same evaluation as those of his customer managers:

- What is his return-to-investment ratio as a comanager of customer funds? As a manager of his own company's funds?
- How do the outcomes that he comanages compare with best practices among his in-company peers? Among his competitors?
- What is his "re-up rate" for customer reinvestment in his next comanaged project? His downtimes between proj-ects?

A customer-client is for growing, not grazing or stripping. Customers are natural resources. As such, they must be nur-tured by farming. By cultivating their fertility to grow funds, they can become an evergreen source of capital infusion for their suppliers. Under comanagement, a reversal of fortune occurs in the concept of the food chain. In each partnership, each coman-ager and customer-client feed the other instead of feeding on each other.

In SalesWorld 2000, old cliches take on new meanings. The comanager's version of "Do I have a deal for you!" is a measur-able improvement in a customer manager's profit contribution, not a price offer on products in oversupply. An offer that a cus-tomer-client cannot refuse is an enhancement of his or her com-petitiveness, not something that is "new and improved!" "Never before!" and a "For the first time!" marvel of the technician's laboratory or the manufacturer's wholly automated line or the service provider's promotion department.

Comanagement is a caring role. Unless comanagers come naturally to it, they must be trained to give care. In business partnerships, care is shown not by concern or interest but by results. Care is an outcome rather than an intent. All comanager training should start with optimal outcomes and work its way back to the most cost-effective strategies to realize them. With this kind of outcome-driven education, comanagers can initiate every profit project with their customers' satisfaction already built in.

Part III

Branding Your Differentiation

How to Seize Primacy as Comanagers by Accelerating Customer Growth

10

The Evaluation of Comanager Competitiveness

Comanagement is transforming the features-and-benefits basis of traditional selling into a comparison of costs with their benefits in terms of reduced operating expenses or increased revenue. Because the costs-and-benefits basis for doing business transforms a comanager's product from a flow of goods and services to a flow of cash, comanagers become economically consequential to their customer-clients. The new streams of cash flow that they account for in a customer's business are the criterion of the performance and timeliness of delivery of their product. Just-in-time means payback on schedule. On spec means that year one cash flow is on plan.

The products and services that make up a comanager's profit projects must, as always, perform according to their operating specifications. Their performance, however, is not the final measurement of a project's success. They are enablers; they are not what is being invested in by a customer but contributors to his or her return on investment by the way they help in the generation of new revenues or help to save costs.

Comparing Profit Projects and Their Comanagers

The benefits of profit projects that propose to save costs are easier to quantify than benefits from revenue projects. Costs are clear-cut. They are internal, not somewhere "out there" in a market where potential revenues must be sought. They are, therefore, more easily measured and controlled. So it is not surprising that most initial and many subsequent profit projects under comanagement focus on cost reduction.

Customer operating costs that are reduced prove that comanagement is working. They make product-by-product evaluation unnecessary. As long as the cash flow from saved costs is on plan and on time for each profit project, a comanager is doing his or her job—actually, he or she is doing half the job, since the other and more difficult half of revenue generation also must be done.

Unlike a majority of cost projects, revenue projects are rarely no-brainers. It is relatively simple for a customer to invest $500,000 today for an annual reduction of $150,000, repeated year after year, in his operation's labor content or scrap or downtime. The calculation of the investment's rate of return when its three-to-five-year cash flows are added up in the form of their net value today is child's play. The customer knows at a high level of confidence how much he can earn on each dollar of investment, when his investment will be paid back, and how much he will make on it.

No such certainty exists for revenue projects since revenues are potential, not actual like costs. No one can be sure how much or how soon new cash will flow into a customer's business on the basis of any initiative to poke, prod, or provoke a market. Too many uncontrollable variables make revenue forecasting a thankless task. Yet precisely because this is so, the tiebreaker for competitive evaluation of comanagers is their performance as revenue generators—in other words, as growers of their customer-clients' businesses.

No matter how much cost you cut out of a customer's operations and no matter how much nonvalue you remove from his systems by integrating them or how many efficiencies you introduce by re-engineering them, you add nothing to the customer's ability to differentiate his business to his own customers. This depends on growing their revenue base.

The combination of increasing a customer-client's revenue base while reducing the cost base that supports his lines of business is the ideal concept of mission for comanagers. Yet inevitably they will be known by their success as rainmakers of revenues.

In the same way that a customer's selection among competitive profit projects can be formulated by using a profit index, comanagers also can be compared. Their profit index is a ratio of the net present value from revenue projects to their investment:

$$\frac{\text{Net Present Value of Expected Benefits From Revenue Projects}}{\text{Investment}}$$

If a comanager's track record in generating new revenues from the customer's market segment with offerings in a similar category is $132,000,000 over the past twelve months and the investment to realize the return was $100,000,000, his profit index is 1.32. This allows his normal productivity as a revenue grower—his *norm*—to be compared against his competitors within the market niche of the customer's business. In this way, the best-in-class comanager can be pinpointed on a per-market per-project basis.

If comanagers are going to be able to prevent commoditization, they must create a brandable differentiation according to their norms, which are the only reliable indicators of potential future performance. Otherwise, it is too easy for customers to use a commodity rule: Invest in anybody who can yield a positive net present value.

When a customer can no longer increase his net present value by substituting one comanager for another, the customer has found his partner. The comanager's norms will have brought them together. Improving his norms by continuously improving the customer's competitive performance will keep them together.

Customer-Driving Your Comanager Choice

Comanagers are positioned to be the correlates of their customer-client partners. A comanager's moment of truth comes when he or she sits side by side with a customer manager—a far cry from face-to-face confrontational selling—and, together, they create new business opportunities or solve business problems in the virtual reality provided by Mack Hanan's software program PIPWARE™. They each bring their own value to the party. The customer manager knows his or her operation. The comanager must know how to improve its profit contribution. Together, they form an ideal growth team.

Comanagers and their customer-clients are united in their objective: to make the customer manager a better competitor—or to say the same thing another way, a better performer as an innovator if he is in R&D or as a processor if he is in manufacturing. The objective they hold in common drives their partnership. Just as the comanager's strategies must serve the customer's objective, so the comanager's skills, characteristics, and competencies must be responsive to his customer's requirements for partnering.

Your choice of comanagers must be driven by the customer managers with whom they are going to have to correlate. If your comanagers come from a customer management background, they will have to be trained to be consultative—that is, co-relative—instead of managerially directive, to be influencers rather than leaders. Comanagers who come from your sales force must also be trained to be consultative. In addition, they will have to be educated in the customer-manager skills, characteristics, and competencies that they must allow themselves to be driven by. As dangerous as it can be to generalize, it is also useful to acknowledge that a customer-manager model exists whose exceptions prove, rather than invalidate, the rule.

Customer managers, whether they operate profit-centered lines of business or cost-centered support functions, are better learners than teachers. When they teach, they teach by example. They are open to learn the same way from their comanagers. They are impatient to implement, conscious of time pressure, and aware of the transient nature of their products and services, their markets, and their own positions in their businesses—even their businesses themselves. They are open to seizing advantages that can be made available to them by their comanagers.

Unlike traditional selling, where the longer a decision to

buy could be postponed, the lower the price of an eventual purchase became, customer managers make decisions fast. The
more autonomous they are, the faster they can move as soon as
they have calculated the gain on one hand, the risk on the other,
and see that they can come out ahead. If they are not born as
competitors, they become that way. Their comanagers must
come to work with them prepared to play without much warm-
up. Few practice shots are allowed.

Customer managers are good at keeping several balls in the
air at once. As long as it affects a priority area of their performance, they can always accommodate one more Profit Improvement Proposal. The only way to get their attention is to link up
with one of their priorities. Everything else becomes "Mickey
Mouse," a distraction of their attention or a dilution of their
funds that must be avoided or evaded. A comanager who seems
to be taking a manager's eye off the ball becomes a competitor,
no longer a partner.

Conversing Predictably With Comanagers

Whether you "Tier 1" your business by becoming a brain shop
that integrates or restructures customer operations, or manages
them in whole or in part as an outsource or a distributor, everything depends on the quality of your comanagers. All the usual
ways of evaluating their competitiveness apply: Are they or can
they become economically consequential to their customer-
clients, are they comfortable thinking of themselves as creators
of incremental cash flows, are they credible investment advisors,
and can they take and hold norm leadership?

An additional way of evaluating comanagement competitiveness is conversational, asking predictive questions like these:

- *How do you react to spending your working hours in high-risk
  situations where you are always on the line?* The comanager
  you want is prepared to accept high risk in return for high
  reward. The reward motivates him or her far more than
  the risk.
- *What is your basis for respecting someone you work with day*

in and day out? The comanager you want respects his or her business partners primarily for their accomplishments. He or she is results-oriented, demanding success in return for respect.

- *What is the single most important attribute that a business partner can praise you for?* The comanager you want seeks to be praised as someone who makes his or her customer manager a leading competitor, someone who is best-in-class and becomes well known for best practices that the comanager has helped install.
- *When you start up a project and you see that it is getting off on the wrong foot, what procedure do you follow?* The comanager you want goes off line immediately to evaluate whether the objective or the strategies to achieve it are at fault, makes any changes that are necessary quickly and decisively, without embarrassment or apology, and goes back to work.
- *How do you react when someone suggests an innovative approach in an area of your professional expertise or knocks down one of your own innovative solutions?* The comanager you want is open to "buy" new ideas. He is able to subordinate his recommendations to the success of a partnered solution. No approach is held sacred. Change and challenge are regarded as learning experiences that add to a comanager's value and inspire him or her to continuously upgrade the stock-in-hand of standard solutions.
- *How do you work with a workaholic partner?* The comanager you want gets up an hour earlier, stays an hour later, and tries to keep one cycle of decisionmaking ahead of his or her customer partner.

Focusing Comanagers on the Main Chance

Comanagers are continually under their customer partners' guns to account for themselves. "Where is your contribution?" is a customer manager's implicit question to anyone who claims partnership privileges, "Where do I look for you in the results?" In the back of his mind, a customer is always nagged by two concerns: (1) Am I really doing this myself? (2) Could I be better off with someone else?

If these concerns migrate to the front of a customer-client's mind, a comanager becomes a former comanager.

A comanager's main chance is to initiate and help see through to conclusion a continuous series of measurable profit contributions. Each of the words in this statement of mission is important: *initiate, see through to conclusion, continuous series,* and *measurable profit contributions.*

In order to fulfill their main chance, your comanagers must focus on three critical success factors that can ensure their competitiveness:

1. Comanagers must score. They must be able to come up with profit projects that they can get approved and funded almost on a one-to-one basis. Failures leave gaps in a customer's continuous improvement, which endangers competitiveness.

2. Comanagers must concentrate on projects that combine two elements: highest profit contribution commensurate with low risk. This means that they should avoid no-brainers with low reward and blockbusters with unacceptably high risk. If home runs are going to be hit, comanagers need to have the forbearance to let their customer-clients hit them. For comanagers, steady and dependable productivity is required with no surprises.

3. Comanagers must plan, propose, and partner each profit project on a short time cycle. Owing to the time value of money, profit improvement is perishable. The value of profits contributed today is always greater than the value of the same profits produced tomorrow. Gaining an investment from a customer manager only begins the comanagement process. Gaining the reinvestment of the profits it produces is the comanager's ongoing task.

The comanager's magic is *to produce short-term results over the long term without prejudicing the long term.*

To sum up these three factors, the premium in comanagement is on speed and consistency to make profit improvement happen as quickly and repeatedly as possible. Fast short-term results meet the criteria on which businesses are judged and by which their managers' performance is evaluated. They are therefore the way comanager competitiveness is evaluated. Without fast, short-term results, no comanager in SalesWorld 2000 can count on being around long enough to be evaluated.

Index